2-
2007

A Blessing and a Curse

of related interest

Pretending to be Normal
Living with Asperger's Syndrome
Liane Holliday Willey
Foreword by Tony Attwood
ISBN 978 1 85302 749 9

The Complete Guide to Asperger's Syndrome
Tony Attwood
ISBN 978 1 84310 495 7

Finding a Different Kind of Normal
Misadventures with Asperger Syndrome
Jeanette Purkis
Foreword by Donna Williams
ISBN 978 1 84310 416 2

Freaks, Geeks and Asperger Syndrome
A User Guide to Adolescence
Luke Jackson
Foreword by Tony Attwood
ISBN 978 1 84310 098 0

A Blessing and a Curse

Autism and Me

Caiseal Mór

Jessica Kingsley Publishers
London and Philadelphia

First published in 2007
by Jessica Kingsley Publishers
116 Pentonville Road
London N1 9JB, UK
and
400 Market Street, Suite 400
Philadelphia, PA 19106, USA

www.jkp.com

Library of Congress Cataloging in Publication Data
A CIP catalog record for this book is available from the Library of Congress

British Library Cataloguing in Publication Data
A CIP catalogue record for this book is available from the British Library

ISBN 978 1 84310 573 2

Printed and bound in the United States by Thomson-Shore, Inc.

Foreword

International bestselling novelist, Caiseal Mór, was born into a larger than life 1960s family and diagnosed as autistic in childhood. His book captures the nostalgic romanticism of the Australian bush in the 1960s but also the deep ignorance and the culture of 'see no evil' in which almost all who could and should have changed things, looked the other way. Assessed as severely brain damaged, then progressively labelled behaviourally disturbed and psychotic before being diagnosed as autistic, all looked the other way as he was brutalised, neglected and traumatised into a range of co-morbid disorders – such abuse even sanctioned by the family doctor.

But Caiseal's book is as beautiful and magical as it is shocking and movingly honest as he takes the reader beyond childhood into a surreal existence as an international traveller, perilous adventurer, and seeker. Caiseal's book is a mirror held up to the most ugly and the most valuable things life can show and offer us and this makes it an important book not only to those involved with autistic or deeply disturbed or abused children, but to those inspired by the resilience of the human spirit.

Those who have appreciated international bestsellers like *Nobody Nowhere*, *Forrest Gump* and *Sybil*, will be inspired by Caiseal's story and transported to a deeply spiritual, philosophical understanding of how a feral autistic child can survive the almost unsurvivable and yet thrive to become such an exceptional and exceptionally multi talented empathic individual.

Donna Williams, renowned autistic author,
artist and autism consultant

Preface

It was a difficult decision to share my story with the world. For years I hid the early draft of this manuscript while I worked up the courage to show it to anyone. In the end what persuaded me to go ahead and publish was the hope that the circumstances of my life might be a source of inspiration to others.

I believe every negative can be turned into a positive. The only trick to it is learning how to see the potential for a positive outcome in the most challenging of situations. I also believe that each of us has the power to change our lives for the better and to make our dreams come true.

My heartfelt thanks go to all at Jessica Kingsley Publishers, especially Jessica Stevens and Lizzie Cox. I also wish to thank all those who've read and commented on my blog in the lead up to this publication. Your support has been very much appreciated.

Last, but by no means least, I'd like to thank my wife, Helen, for her patience, understanding and acceptance of me and my strange ways. I'm also extremely grateful to her for the wonderful portrait she painted for the front cover of this book.

For those who'd like to know more about me and my work, my blog can be found at http://mahjee.blogspot.com and my website is www.mahjee.com.

One

I've been a zombie. I've marched among the ranks of the walking dead. For a long while I muddled through my restless existence enshrouded within a thick, heavy fog of dreamy amnesia. I was lost to the world. Every now and then I might snatch a brief glimpse of my surroundings, but it was never enough to break the powerful spell that bound me.

Mostly I've been so shut down I didn't know who I was, what I was doing or where I was going. Whenever circumstances overwhelmed me I lapsed into a crippling catatonic state that could last for hours or days. Until three years ago when the enchantment began to lift, I was mostly ignorant of my predicament. As I stirred from my weird, stumbling slumber I began to look at the world through new eyes.

I don't fit the clichéd stereotype of autism. I'm not physically disabled. I'm not deaf, dumb or blind. I don't stutter uncontrollably. Nor do I compulsively twitch and cower. I'm not the Rain Man, for pity's sake. If it weren't for my eccentric fashion sense I probably wouldn't stand out in the crowd at all.

In my humble opinion autism is a wondrous gift – a blessing of sorts. As far as I'm concerned, autistic benefits far outstrip any drawbacks you can imagine. But it's taken me a lifetime of self-examination and inquiry to arrive at that conclusion.

Parents, peers and psychologists made sure I knew I was a defective child. I was very young when I adopted the view that I'm of less value than everybody else. It's a view I've been unable to shake. I've long accepted that I'm a deeply flawed individual, inherently faulty and, therefore, not quite human. It was drummed into me day and night: reinforce an assertion to someone enough times and eventually they won't question it.

My resulting sense of unworthiness was reinforced through the excessive use of a powerful tool known as shame. These days I regard shame as a weapon of mass destruction in the battle for conformity. I know that if I'm ever to heal the splintered pieces of myself I must first stare down the dragon of my shame and subdue him; even if the blood-sucker can't be slain.

My original intention in putting all this down on paper was to release the terrible burden of shame from my shoulder. What I've discovered is that real shame – regularly reinforced, industrial strength, 60 gigahertz shame – doesn't just melt away with a mumbled confession. That sort of shame is a wicked little beastie who digs his claws in deep. He stays forever close, clinging tightly to your back no matter how much you squirm and struggle.

I often dream of a time when the shame-dragon was not my constant companion. In my dream I'm four years old or thereabouts, in the days before I spoke my first words. I'm seated at my bedroom window staring at a tall gum tree outside in the empty paddock. The tropical night air is heavy in the stifling humidity of the Australian summer. Suddenly an intense white flash briefly parts the darkness. The dry top-branches of the tree burst into flame, exploding like an enormous Roman candle. I love the scent of burning eucalyptus oil. Fearlessly I run outside to bathe my spirit in the brilliant orange light of the burning tree.

That vivid dream still visits me at least once a week. I believe it may hold a clue to my mystery. I get great satisfaction from discovering hidden meanings in messages. I love deciphering symbols and secret signs. I could spend all day joining the dots if I was allowed to. Perhaps that's why I was drawn to the craft of the storyteller.

Storytelling has been the most satisfying experience of my strange life. I regard it as a kind of spiritual practice akin to meditation. I'm told I've got a gift for it. So to begin with I'd like to share one of my favourite tales with you.

There was this young man I used to follow around from time to time. His name was Marco. Marco Polo. Marco Polo was me.

A battered old yellow taxi coughed, grinding to a halt in a choking dust cloud. The Moroccan in the front seat turned around smiling. His bright blue eyes didn't fit with his tar-stained teeth, coffee-complexion and curly black hair. He was a halfblood.

'We've come to the frontier, my friend,' he stated in his thick, almost comical, French accent. 'All you need to do is present your passport to the guards and you'll be on your way back to Spain.'

His passenger was a young, wide-eyed traveller with golden hair shaved close to the scalp. His eyes were almost exactly the same blue as those of his Moroccan friend. He stared off out the window and did not reply.

'Marco? Did you hear me?'

'Thank you,' the young man managed to stutter as he stirred from his private world. 'I heard you.' His eyebrow twitched and his hands were shaking.

Even though it was a dry, hot day Marco was wearing a thick, dark-blue coat that had once been a Royal Marines dress-uniform jacket. He'd bought it in Carnaby Street in London. Marco was an eclectic collector of strange artefacts. He had a slender bag slung over his shoulder that held his few meagre possessions.

His latest acquisitions were a garish Moroccan carpet he'd bought for 50 English pounds. His Moroccan friend had given him a traditional Berber jalabah – the long, hooded robe favoured by the people of the Atlas mountains. It was woven from camel hair and it smelled like shit.

'Are you ready, Marco?' the Moroccan asked. 'You must go now or you'll miss the ferry to Spain.'

Marco hesitated. He slipped a hand into his pocket brushing the large lump of hashish that had also been a gift from his friend. The taxi driver turned around and frowned.

'What are you waiting for?'

Marco swung the door open and as he was about to step out his Moroccan friend grabbed him firmly on the wrist. Marco instantly recoiled, snatching his arm away.

'Don't take a bus to the port,' the Moroccan advised. He handed Marco a small amount of money. 'It's too dangerous. Take this. Find a taxi.

Travel alone if you can. Trust no one. Morocco is a bad place. There are bad people everywhere.'

Marco accepted the banknote with a nod. His manner was very formal and stilted like some character out of a 1930s film.

'You have been very good to me,' he replied. 'I hope I can repay you someday.'

'You've already repaid me by accepting my hospitality and my gift.'

Then the Moroccan added something in Arabic that Marco didn't understand.

'What did you say?'

His friend repeated the phrase then explained the meaning.

'God is great.'

'Allah Akbar,' Marco mimicked precisely.

The Moroccan's mouth dropped open. He was shocked and suddenly unsettled.

'Do you speak Arabic?'

'I'm good with languages,' Marco explained, modestly. 'Good-bye.'

'Farewell.'

Marco got out of the car and headed toward the frontier crossing, dodging between the camels and the hawkers selling cheap tourist trinkets. He joined the queue of people waiting to cross the border on foot. There were thirty or so travellers ahead of him in the line.

He took the time to take in his surroundings. There were soldiers lined up along the border fence on the Moroccan side. They were spaced about six paces apart and they all had their rifles pointed at the Spanish soldiers on the opposite side.

Ahead of him in the queue a fight broke out. There was a scuffle and some yelling. Half a dozen soldiers appeared. They dragged a man away to a waiting car. He fought them every inch of the way, shrieking in Arabic to anyone who'd listen. The man was beaten to the ground and kicked repeatedly. By the time they'd bundled him into the car he was unconscious.

Marco's heart beat in his throat; he swallowed hard. His instincts told him he was in terrible danger. His fingers found the block of hashish in his pocket. It was half the size of a golf ball. It hadn't struck him before that moment that carrying drugs over an international frontier was a risky business. He began to regret accepting the generous gift.

His throat was dry. Marco was sweating. A Moroccan border guard strolled along the line and stopped directly in front of him. The soldier took a few moments to look him over. He touched the sleeve of Marco's blue coat.

'Bonjour, Napoleon,' the soldier quipped, laughing at his own joke.

Another border guard appeared, drawn by the blue coat. Marco pulled away while the two soldiers sniggered derisively. To anyone observing the scene it might have seemed as if Marco was standing up to the bullies, but the truth was he was scared half out of his wits. The soldiers moved on to harass a young American woman further down the line who was travelling alone. Marco breathed a little easier.

As soon as the soldiers were gone he began a debate with himself. He knew hashish was perfectly legal in Morocco. He reasoned that his friend hadn't realised the dangers involved in taking it over the border. Marco reminded himself that he didn't even like drugs.

'What am I doing here?' he asked himself aloud.

The old man in front of him turned around and frowned.

'What's happening?' he asked in Spanish.

'Nada.'

Marco tried to appear calm but he was twitching again. The old man squinted, spat and shrugged. By then there were only twenty people between him and the window where the officer was stamping passports.

'What am I going to do?' Marco stuttered, immediately biting his tongue so he wouldn't say anything more.

The old man heard him but didn't bother turning around again.

Marco didn't want to offend his Moroccan friend by discarding the generous gift. But he was frightened of what might happen to him if he was caught with such a large quantity of hashish. He knew the Spanish authorities were cracking down on anyone caught possessing the drug. Torn between loyalty to his friend and his own safety, Marco came to a difficult decision.

He slipped a hand into his pocket, grabbed the hashish and, as discreetly as possible, he dropped it on the ground at his feet. In the next breath he heard a shuffle behind him, turned and saw the man behind him bend over to pick it up. The Moroccan sniffed the block, smiled and sighed, 'Allah Akbar.' Then he calmly placed it in his pocket and tenderly patted it.

When Marco stepped up to the window to have his passport stamped he was visibly shaken. The officer seated behind the glass took his papers and examined them carefully. He turned to consult someone who was out of sight in the darkness of the room beyond.

'I don't like drugs,' Marco spurted. 'I don't have any drugs on me.'

The officer turned his attention back to Marco, opened the passport again and leafed through every page one by one at a leisurely pace. He examined the photo, looked into Marco's eyes and smiled. But it wasn't a pleasant kind of smile. It was a knowing smile; a smile that said, 'I've got you!'

All of a sudden the smile fell away. Marco's heart stopped.

'Pass,' the officer declared sharply.

He stamped a page and pushed the document under the window.

'I don't have any drugs,' Marco insisted.

'Pass!' the officer shouted; his thumb emphatically indicating toward the Spanish side of the frontier.

Marco took his papers and walked off toward the waiting buses. He was still in shock. He was so relieved to have got through the border post without incident he hardly noticed how much his legs were shaking. He only made it twenty paces before he stumbled and fell on his knees in the dust.

A bus driver ran up and helped him to his feet. The kindly man dusted Marco off and held a hand out to indicate his bus. Marco recoiled, stepping out of reach. The bus driver frowned in confusion.

'Are you going to the port?' he asked in Spanish.

'Si.'

The bus driver moved to help Marco with his bag. Marco stepped away again quickly.

'I'll take a taxi.'

'Sure?'

'Si. Gracias.'

In the next moment three men in scruffy brown suits appeared behind Marco.

'Taxi?' one of them asked as he touched the traveller on the shoulder.

Marco nodded. They led him to a waiting car, but Marco's instincts told him something was wrong. He looked at the driver. The man was unshaven and he had the distinct high cheekbones of a gypsy.

Marco's Spanish friends had warned him many times about the gypsies — in Spanish they're called *gitanos*. Don't trust them, they'd warned. They're the worst kind of thieves. They slit the throats of their victims and leave them to die. Stay away from *gitanos*.

Marco halted in his tracks.

'No, gracias,' he stuttered, but even as he spoke two of the men grabbed him under the arms and bundled him into the car. Before he could protest, the third man was seated in the front and Marco was stuck between two strangers in the back.

In the next instant the man in the front seat pulled out a knife and waved the point in Marco's face. Despite the heat Marco's skin turned icy cold as all the blood in his body froze.

'Silence,' was all the man said.

The car sped off along the road to the port leaving a trail of dust in its wake. Marco hung his head, staring at his hands in his lap, unable to look up.

So it had come to this, he thought. He'd always expected to die young, but he was sad because he felt he'd just started to get the hang of life. He'd found a place where he was accepted for who he was. He had friends who cared about him. They treated him like family. He had a wonderful job.

'What a pity it has to end this way,' he noted aloud with detachment.

'Silence!'

The car left the main road and wound its way up to a little village on the side of a hill. When it came to a halt the *gitanos* dragged Marco out with his bag still over his shoulder.

'If you're going to kill me, could you make it quick?' he calmly asked the man with the knife.

'Silence!'

Moments later they had him in a back alley of the village. One of them went through his bag on the cobbles. Another kept watch while the man with the knife pressed the point to Marco's throat.

'Mon Dieu,' the young traveller sighed, surprised he'd remembered that phrase. Then he added, 'Allah Akbar.' That was the closest Marco ever came to a prayer. He thought it wise to say something like that in his last moments just in case there was a God after all.

The *gitano* stepped back and gestured menacingly with the knife.

'Where is it?'

Marco took out his passport and handed the document over. The *gitano* touched his knife to the silver ring that hung around Marco's neck on a fine silver chain. It had been a gift from a girlfriend in Australia. Until that moment he'd forgotten he was wearing it; the same way he'd forgotten all about her.

The *gitano* snatched the chain with his free hand and snapped it. Then he greedily stuffed both ring and chain into his pocket. Once again he raised the knife point as he carefully went through Marco's pockets with his free hand methodically turning them out.

There were handfuls of seashells and red stones. There were brass buttons and tiny pieces of shattered windscreen. A selection of brightly coloured embroidery thread, some feathers, scraps of parchment; a little box of pen nibs for calligraphy. All were unceremoniously scattered across the cobbled street.

But the *gitano* didn't find the 100 Swiss francs sewn into the left arm of the blue jacket. Or the English 20 pound note concealed in the right.

'You're not very good at this, are you?' Marco noted when the thief had finished.

'Shut up!'

The *gitano* started rummaging through Marco's pockets again. In that instant a teenage boy suddenly appeared in the lane. He stopped dead in his tracks when he saw what was happening.

'Could you help me, please?' Marco stuttered, raising a finger to get the boy's attention.

The knife point pressed into his neck, nicking the skin.

'Silence!'

The boy ran off in terror. The three robbers were obviously upset. They spoke sharply to one another in a strange language Marco had never heard before. An argument broke out. The one with the knife was shouting at the other two. Suddenly he turned and placed the blade up under Marco's ear. It was clear he was about to slit his victim's throat.

'Allah Akbar,' the *gitano* sneered, preparing to spill blood. His sarcasm was lost on Marco.

Before he had a chance to make the cut a large group of men appeared. The boy who'd run off was talking above the shouts of the villagers. The *gitanos* instantly turned tail and ran in the opposite direction.

The crowd of men raised their voices and sprinted after the thieves with fists flailing and curses flying.

Marco felt as if he'd been caught up in a whirlwind. Before he knew what had happened, he found himself seated at a table in a house. A cup of sweet, steaming mint tea was placed before him. There was a lot of shouting in the streets outside.

An old grey-bearded man arrived triumphantly holding aloft the stolen passport. He was dressed in a brown Berber jalabah exactly the same as Marco's. He took a long while to sift through the document without saying a word while he calmly sipped a cup of mint tea. At last he tossed the passport down on the table before Marco.

'Go home, fool,' he said in an educated, upper-class English accent. 'You don't belong here. Why did you come to this country anyway?'

'I'm a traveller.'

'You're a bloody fool.'

'What are you doing here?' Marco stuttered.

'I'm rescuing you, it would seem,' the old man replied.

The rest of Marco's belongings were quickly retrieved and spread out on the table in front of him. He reached out and clutched the ring to his heart. Everything was there, except his most precious items, the shells, stones, pieces of glass and all the assorted treasures he'd been collecting for years. And one other thing was gone – his ticket for the ferry back to Spain.

There was more shouting outside. The three *gitanos* were dragged up the street with their arms bound behind their backs at the elbows.

'Anything missing?' the old man asked.

Marco explained about the ticket.

'Don't worry, we'll take care of that.'

While the *gitanos* were being stood up against a wall the old man shoved Marco's belongings into his shoulder bag. Then he led him out on to the street. As Marco turned the corner the villagers began pelting the thieves with stones in a huge hail that brought all three to their knees in the first seconds.

The old man bundled Marco into a waiting taxi.

'What's happening?'

'We can't let those bastards get away with it. We've got to send a clear message that this sort of behaviour won't be tolerated.'

'Thank you for taking care of me.'

'Luck is with you, my friend,' he declared, with a smile. I'll never forget the way he said that. It was so old-fashioned and surreal. 'When you get to the port a man from the village will give you a ticket for the next ferry. I advise you not to miss that boat. If you stay in Africa tonight you may live to regret it.'

Marco promised he'd catch the ferry. He arrived at the port, was given his ticket, and boarded the ship just in time. On the ferry he met a pair of German lads who were travelling by motorcycle. They offered him a lift on the back of one of their bikes to the coastal town where Marco had been staying.

At midnight, after a hair-raising ride up the winding coast road towards Malaga, Marco was dropped off outside the youth hostel where he'd been working and living for three months. The front door was locked, so he slipped the jalabah over his head and curled up to sleep in a corner.

For a long while he couldn't manage to calm down enough to sleep. He'd gone off to Morocco in search of adventure and he'd certainly got plenty of that. Marco laughed. The whole experience had been like something out of a Humphrey Bogart movie. He lay there looking up at the stars, grateful to be back on familiar ground.

'Allah Akbar,' he repeated, over and over under his breath.

Eventually, not long after dawn, Marco drifted off into a fitful sleep. He dreamt about a flaming gum tree.

Eyes open.
Heart asleep.
The eyes only see what they want to.
I want to live this mystery with my heart awake.
My eyes see nothing when they sleep
But my heart has many eyes.
And I sleep much better when my heart's awake.

How's this for symmetry? It was 23 years ago when I went to Morocco. I was 23 years old at the time. I don't know about you, but I find symmetry extremely satisfying.

I've always been a bit slow on the uptake and I was unbelievably gullible in those days. I'm still very naïve – perhaps these days I'm a little more careful and less trusting. Back then, if someone was friendly to me, they were also automatically my friend and deserved my trust.

It was only recently that I pieced together all the elements of that bizarre string of incidents. I came to a startling realisation. My Moroccan friend hadn't given me a block of hashish because he liked me. I was his delivery boy. The *gitanos* were waiting for me on the Spanish side of the frontier to receive the package. It took me 23 years to work that out. I told you I can be slow on the uptake.

I began my story with that incident because it was a major turning point. It split my life into two distinct parts. Everything that happened before the knife touched me under the ear was the first half. The division of my life into two equal portions is quite a magical coincidence but it's not as remarkable as some of the other happy accidents I've been involved in.

Consider this. At midday I was crossing the frontier into Spanish Morocco – an unwitting drug courier; risking imprisonment or perhaps death. By midnight I was curled up safe and sound on the porch of the youth hostel, wrapped in a brown Berber jalabah that stank of camel-shit, an odour I now find very reassuring.

I don't know about you, but I call that a bloody miracle. And it was all the more miraculous because, though I didn't realise it at the time, that incident set off another series of miracle-dominoes that altered the course of my life journey.

For a long time after I returned to Spain I was in a state of wonderful exhilaration. I felt like a new person; as if my spirit had been washed clean. My little adventure in Morocco set me on a path I'm still walking today.

As I looked up to the stars that night I became convinced I had to radically reinvent myself; wipe the slate clean and start again from scratch. I set my sights on getting a university education. I decided that if I was ever going to be healed I would have to shed my skin and move on.

What would he need to be healed of, you might ask. He's had 12 novels published. He's travelled the world as a free spirit. He's had adventures other folks only dream of. He's a musician, painter and sculptor. He could have done anything he wanted with his life. He's so successful, so confident, so relaxed.

Such observations have often been made by folks who don't know me very well. As far as I'm concerned, those descriptions are as incomplete as all the negative ones I've been lumbered with. Psycho, retard, schizophrenic, sociopath; I've heard them all.

To look at me you'd probably never guess I'm so strange. I've learned to cover my strangeness quite well, most of the time. It's not hard to hide yourself when you don't get close to other people in the first place.

Apart from the last few years, I've lived mostly as an extreme recluse. I've always had a deep ambivalence toward people. On the one hand, I yearn to be close to others. Like anyone else I have a burning desire to be held and to feel loved. On the other hand, I hate being touched. I get little comfort from being physically close to others. The accompanying sensations are too overwhelming. The emotions that are invoked threaten to overtake me; so I get frightened. Proximity is something I may endure because I want to express respect and love for an individual; but I'm never, ever, comfortable with it.

It's a feature of who I am. I like to be alone. I prefer to be by myself. I'm led to believe it's one of the symptoms that mark me as autistic; though it's fairly certain trauma has a lot to do with my reclusive nature. I'm of the opinion psychologists play a bit of a guessing game when it comes to autism.

In my case, autism certainly wasn't the first conclusion the learned doctors jumped to. There were a few other significant stabs in the dark before that.

My early childhood has always been a bit of a blur, so when I got curious about my origins I had to do some research on myself. Before Mother passed away, 15 years ago, I had a few opportunities to speak with her. In one of our final conversations she revealed some facts about my early life that I hadn't previously been aware of.

I was an unusually quiet baby. Within a few days of my birth the doctors realised there was something very wrong with me. I had no obvious physical defects but I wasn't responding to stimuli. According to these experts, that meant I was severely brain damaged.

I wasn't expected to live. Mother was told to expect the worst. As a result, even though I was an extremely beautiful child – some said angelic – she never allowed herself to become attached to me.

In my first few years I rarely cried or made a sound – not even when, at 18 months, I rolled my pram down the stairs and cut my forehead. After that tumble I quietly crawled off and went about my baby business with blood dripping off my chin.

In my second year I suddenly stood up on my own two feet for the first time and ran. Mother reckoned it was as if I'd been biding my time, waiting my chance to escape. We were in the city on a shopping expedition. I leapt out of my pram when she wasn't looking and sprinted off down the street as fast as my little legs could carry me. I crossed dangerously close in front of a tram and disappeared into the crowd, tearing my clothes off as I went.

I would have got clean away too, if I hadn't run straight into the arms of an enormous fluffy panda bear that hugged me so tight I couldn't move. I opened my mouth wide struggling to scream; but nothing came out. I hadn't started speaking at that stage.

That panda bear is still very vivid in my mind – the man in the panda suit haunted my nightmares and my waking life for years afterwards. He was very angry with me. I'd knocked over all the free samples of potato crisps he was giving out. His wares were scattered over the pavement.

I remember him holding on to me, even though I squirmed desperately to get away. Then, suddenly, he was laughing. The change was so terrifying I froze, stiff as a board. My bowels turned to water, spilling runny shit down my legs. I vomited up my breakfast porridge and he pushed me away in disgust.

Mother said she caught up with me at that very moment. She smacked me hard across the backside again and again until I fell over. No matter how hard she hit me I didn't make a sound. I ended up naked on my back on the pavement with my arms tight by my sides and my legs straight. I was staring up into the sky with my unblinking eyes wide open.

It cost her ten shillings to replace the potato crisps – an enormous amount to a struggling family in those days. She never trusted me again and never forgave me to her dying day for the awful embarrassment I caused her. Whenever we went anywhere after that I was put on a leather dog-leash secured under my arms and around my chest.

Soon after that incident my hearing was tested. I remember some of what happened. I had to wear headphones and the loud beeps left my ears ringing painfully. I had all sorts of impressive medical paraphernalia taped to my head. I have a vague recollection of the room. It was dark and I felt safe.

When they left me alone, pretty lights flashed in front of me and a big machine hummed. I liked its song and I loved the colours of the lights. I remember the nurse because she hummed a little melody in tune with the machine.

In my early years I didn't blink very often; if I did, it was mechanical. I often flapped my arms about like a stranded pelican, but I almost always had a blank expression on my face. The sight and sound of steam trains made me clap like a performing seal, and I'm a little embarrassed to admit they still inspire the same delighted reaction.

I knocked cups and plates off the table because I liked the sound of china smashing. I stared endlessly into the mirror. I compulsively licked my lips and picked congealed snot from my nose. Snot was the only thing I voluntarily ate without putting up a fight.

I sat with my head pressed close to the radiogram speakers whenever a record was put on – unless it was fifties jazz. I hated jazz and I'd hide in the closet whenever I heard it. I still get very upset when I hear jazz of that era. It frustrates me and I have to fight a strong compulsion to find a dark place to hide. When there was no music I tapped my feet on the floor creating intricate rhythms.

The doctors couldn't work out exactly what was wrong. It was the sixties and few, if any, medical professionals in Australia had an awareness of autism. The diagnosis, once again, was irreparable brain damage. Mother put me on a waiting list to be permanently admitted to the state mental hospital.

My parents had a house in the outer southern suburbs of Brisbane; the capital city of the sub-tropical state of Queensland. My father's mother, a widow, lived nearby in a poky, two-room, fibro shack. Father's sister, my auntie, lived on a large chicken farm on the other side of a narrow, trickling creek, a stone's throw away.

Auntie was an enthusiastic evangelical Christian. Father often in-sulted her behind her back or told derogatory tales to illustrate her stupidity. There was no love lost between them. Auntie's husband was a tall, dour Scotsman who had more wrinkles than anyone else I knew. They had two children.

Mother's parents shared our house. Everyone called my mother's mother Nanna. Later, she was the first person I ever addressed by name. I hated using names. This quirk is typical of me even today. I still avoid using names whenever possible. When I eventually started talking I called her Nanna because I worked out it was her nickname. That made it okay.

Nanna was a gentle soul who'd had an extremely hard life. Most of her hardship was caused by my grandfather – Pop. She was absent-minded and often fell asleep in the middle of a story or while contentedly chewing her supper. She was made fun of for being slow-witted but I liked her more than anyone else in the world. She told marvellous stories.

Pop was a tough, strong, belligerent man whose wiry hands always reeked of tobacco. He had a sun-tanned face with golden blond hair that was only just beginning to grey. He could roll a cigarette with one hand. When I was older I found that fascinating. I learned how to do it. Pop also had a wicked sense of humour; but he could turn violent at the drop of a hat. Nanna blamed the rum for that.

In his time he'd been a blacksmith, a horse-breaker, a cattle-drover, a coal-miner and he'd wielded a cane-knife in the sugar fields. In the early sixties, when mechanical harvesters replaced the cane-cutters, he was reduced to living in the city and working on the wharves unloading ships.

He hated living in Brisbane. He said the place brought back too many painful memories for him. In summary he inhabited a kind of living Hell and he made sure everyone else did too.

In one of our last conversations Mother told me she'd been physically brutalised by Pop as a child. A few times I saw him raise his hand in the air as both Nanna and Mother ran for cover. I believe Pop was behind Mother's propensity for cruelty.

I was lucky. He usually ignored me. Rarely did his gaze fall in my direction. The worst thing I recall that he ever did to me was to stub out his cigarette on my arm and call me an idiot. I didn't cry out. I never cried out. He must have thought that was hilarious because he doubled up with laughter.

I was instinctively very frightened of Pop right from the start. I didn't like anything about him. In fact I hated being in the same room as him. I'd often run outside to escape the sound of his voice. If he gave an order, it was instantly obeyed. He commanded a huge amount of respect. It may have been born of fear but it was respect nonetheless.

Despite my overwhelming fear of the man I was also intrigued by him. His behaviour threw into sharp contrast the weaknesses in Father. The two of them never got along. Pop was always playing nasty little practical jokes on Father.

He'd lift all the lids on the paint tins in the shed then loosen the screws on the shelves so they were balancing precariously. Father would close the shed door behind him and you'd hear the paint tins and the shelves come crashing down. It was clear Pop got a kick out of tormenting Father.

When I was three my little sister was born. I cried for the first time shortly after her arrival. I can't say whether the two developments were in any way related, but I don't see any connection. There was a party the day she was pronounced healthy and normal. I stayed in my room and listened to the glasses clinking; the laughter and the singing. I didn't like crowds. I was overjoyed to be forgotten for the night.

Within a few weeks my whole life was turned upside down. First Nanna and Pop moved into their own housing commission place on the other side of town. I was glad he was gone. What I didn't understand at the time was that Nanna had been my guardian.

Without Nanna to keep watch on her, my mother slipped into neglecting me. Mother had a new focus of interest that took up all her energy. My sister cried all the time to be fed. Mother was always exhausted and cranky.

Father got promoted and had to work longer hours. He'd been accepted into a higher degree of the Masonic Lodge as well. He had more responsibility and privileges. The mood in the house was suddenly much brighter. I heard Father laughing for the first time.

I copied him. I started laughing. I'd laugh the moment my eyes opened in the morning, and sometimes I wouldn't stop even when all the lights went out that night. I'd laugh when Mother slapped me. Much to her embarrassment, I'd point at strangers in the street and laugh.

Mother told everyone I was desperate for attention. She often explained my odd behaviour as jealousy over my sister. That wasn't at all true. Quite the opposite in fact. I was so relieved when my sister came along. I hated attention. I loathed being touched, fondled, spoken to or cooed over. I preferred to be left alone in my room in the quiet. I couldn't work out why no one understood that.

Before my sister I'd been forced to be sociable. She took up my share of the attention and the resulting freedom was joyous. Much of the fear that had haunted me up to that point seemed to melt away.

I never spoke to my sister much. In later years she pretended she didn't know me. Even though we shared a house and family I don't recall ever looking directly at her more than a few times.

Mother became increasingly worried my mental problems might be contagious. She often warned me to stay away from my sister. She needn't have bothered. We were never close. To begin with, I didn't like what I saw. In my eyes she appeared sickly and weak. I had a sense she wasn't going to be around for very long. So I was determined to make the most of her presence while it lasted. While my little sister was being fussed over I could drift off into my own world. I was suddenly free to explore my surroundings.

Two

The family house was a typical timber Queenslander – the living space was raised up on high stilts so the cool air could circulate under the floorboards taking the edge off the oppressive summer heat. My room looked out over the chicken farm, the creek and the little shack Father's mother lived in. Later when I could talk, I called her Nanna-Father. Though I never called her that to her face for fear of a belting.

A lot of my fourth year was spent sitting in my own shit on a wobbly chair at the window contentedly watching the world go by. I loved that chair and I loved the window. I learned a lot looking out at the world.

I loved the cackling chickens on Auntie's farm across the creek. I loved the birds. I loved the sounds of dogs barking in the distance. I loved the pines and the tangled mango. Most of all I loved one towering solitary eucalyptus tree that grew down near the creek about 50 yards away.

I watched it by day. I watched it by night. It had a long, slender grey trunk that was always shedding great swathes of bark. The gum tree stood in the middle of a cleared space in a little gully near the water. Our house was built on a rise so the leafy crown of the gum was almost exactly level with my window.

When the full moon fell on the trunk it shone like beaten silver. It was one of the most contented trees I've ever met because it always had plenty to drink even when the rains didn't come. Ring-tail possums used to clamber up and down it every night playing out their territorial feuds; one clan against the other. I knew every one of those possums by their individual markings.

Then one evening at the start of summer, the possums didn't come. Just before sunset the tree had been taken over by a big male koala. I'll never forget him. The moon was so bright it lit everything up as clear as day. The gum tree was silvery blue.

With his big ears he looked to me exactly like a grey panda bear. Naturally I was extremely frightened of him at first. He settled into a fork and munched some leaves. I was deeply concerned that he'd come to get me.

When he finished eating he tore off a branch, threw it down and grunted. I was sure I was in deadly danger. Then he suddenly bellowed out a loud, growling, passionate song. My fear fell away immediately.

I was entranced by his voice. Though I didn't understand his words, they touched a deep part of me. Even now, as I'm writing about it, the memory of his song brings tears to my eyes. He was King Koala.

He performed his low, rhythmic chant throughout that first night. Now and then, he'd stop to take a breather but he didn't fall completely silent until after sunrise. It seemed to me that whenever he had a break he'd turn to stare across at my window. King Koala was my first friend and I will love him until the day I die.

In the wee hours Father shouted at him to shut his bloody trap. Mother warned she'd cut his bloody tree down and that'd give him something to sing about. They must have buried their heads in their pillows after that. Hot summer nights in Australia fray tempers and drain the strength out of you. My parents probably couldn't be bothered getting up to chase him off.

For three days the King slept up in the gum tree. I copied him. Between sunrise and sunset I curled up under my mosquito net and hugged the pillow close to me as if it was a branch. How I wanted to be like him. I longed to go off and learn his language. I wanted to be a koala.

On the second night he bellowed again. I ached to answer him but I didn't dare. I was too frightened of the consequences to make even the slightest sound. Under my breath I mimicked his words. I took note of every little nuance. His call was like a wonderful poem to me.

I now know that's exactly what it was – a love poem. He was acting out the koala mating ritual: looking for a female. But I couldn't have known that then.

On the third night the breeze blew up from the gully and I revelled in his strong marsupial scent, something similar to eucalyptus crossed with a hint of freshly turned soil. I've always had a very powerful sense of smell. I found his scent extremely soothing.

It never crossed my mind that he was different from me. I looked up to him like I might have done a big brother; if I'd had one. He was everything I wanted to be. He was free to come and go as he pleased. My parents threatened him but they couldn't touch him. In my heart I begged him to take me away into the bush.

Long after midnight, when the moon had set, I heard another koala calling in the distance. Before dawn the King made his way cautiously down the trunk and skittered off into the bush. I didn't see him go. It was too dark.

He must have been a long way off when he called out again to say farewell. His scent was already dissipating. I crawled under the mosquito net and cried myself to sleep.

The next night I waited to see if he'd return. He didn't. The possums danced around the roots of the tree, chasing their tails and screeching. A tawny frog-mouth owl sat in the high branches calling 'moh-poke'.

I was getting frantic. How could King Koala leave me? Why didn't he take me with him? I sat at the window with my jaw wide, mouthing koala words under my breath.

It must have been about three in the morning when I was finally overwhelmed by grief and loss. Foolishly I put all fear of retribution aside and took in a deep breath. Then I bellowed at the top of my lungs with every bit of force I could muster. Mother later said I sounded exactly like him. She reckoned I set off the dogs barking all over the neighbourhood and I just kept on bellowing. The chickens were screeching. Father called on the Son of God by name. Then he yelled at me to shut up.

The trouble was, once I'd started I couldn't bring myself to stop the flood of sound. Next thing there was a loud noise behind me. My bedroom door was flung open. I turned around, still bellowing.

Father punched me hard in the nose. My koala call was cut short. Then I was lying on my back on the floor. He stood over me for a long while with his hands on his hips staring at me. After a while he tried to pick me up but I fought him off.

He called me a fucking idiot then he went back to bed. I heard my parents whispering in their room for a long while after. When all was silent in the house again I got back up on my chair to look out the window.

I remember this incident so well because that was the night I started speaking. I've always considered my first words to have been of the koala kind. When I was older, people called me a bullshit-artist if I told them about it, so I stopped sharing that story.

Like any skill or craft I've mastered in this life – and there are many – speaking koala was something I passionately wanted to do. So I picked it up quickly.

I believe I slipped into a long period of trance-like behaviour after that. Mother told me that I rarely acknowledged the existence of other human beings. I would silently pull my own hair out at the dinner table or sit rocking back and forth as I hummed one of my own personal melodies that no one else recognised.

Though I may have switched off for a while, I was soon able to convincingly imitate many birdcalls. My skill for mimicry was so finely tuned that the magpies, butcher-birds and currawongs would fly down to the garden to chatter with me. The chickens gathered in a circle to listen intently. I even managed to fool some wise old kookaburras. Within six months I was whistling tunes I'd heard on the radio as well.

In my fifth year Father brought home a black and white television. Mother hated the thing at first; until she realised it was a great baby-sitter. I was locked in a room and sat in front of it most of the day. It absolutely captured my attention. I couldn't take my eyes off it.

I learned so much from that television. It was the second friend I ever had. Before long, rolling strings of gibberish were bubbling out of me. I learned lots of words – words were never a problem with me. The trouble was, I had my own unique way of knitting them together that didn't quite make sense.

I sang the advertising jingles. I hummed the theme tune from the evening news. I often sank so deeply into the dream world of the box that when the television was switched off I'd scream and bawl with frustration. Mother soon discovered it was also the best way to get me to eat.

When I was caught in the trance of the dancing lights and voices I'd shovel food into my mouth like a robot. It was always switched on for breakfast, lunch and dinner. If I was throwing a tantrum, she'd flick the tuner and I'd instantly be silent and submissive.

'That's why they call it the idiot box,' Father used to say.

I was taken to a doctor who said I was severely handicapped and feeble-minded. He said I was a mental vegetable and that I'd never live an independent life. He offered to push me along on the waiting list for the state asylum. There were no special schools in Queensland back then.

In the sixties the public hospital system was free but the waiting list for the asylum was very long. It could take years for a place to come up. My parents were working class so they couldn't afford to put me in a private hospital. That's how I ended up spending so much time with the television.

One day Nanna heard me singing a song. I rarely spoke directly to anyone or looked them in the eye unless they forced me to. When she found out I was repeating a television commercial for fly spray Nanna was furious. She had a terrible fight with Mother over it. Television became a monster I was only allowed to spend a few hours with every day.

I had to find something else to do with my time. If I wasn't kept busy, I very quickly got bored. There wasn't much to do around the house without getting in trouble. I got blamed for everything that went wrong. Mostly I sat on my chair at the window to avoid being the focus of Mother's simmering rage.

As time went on I became less and less satisfied with the view from my window. I wanted to go outside and explore. Occasionally I'd sneak out to press against the gum tree trying to catch a whiff of King Koala's scent. I'd try climbing the gum, but there was nowhere to get a foothold on the smooth trunk. So I settled for the mango tree that grew closer to our house. The twisted branches were low and the broad leaves were so thick I could hide up there in peace for hours. Sometimes I'd watch the world all morning before Mother noticed I was missing.

One day I was up the mango tree when I thought I saw the branch moving. I heard a hissing sound like air escaping from a bicycle tyre. Right beside me on the branch, close enough that I could've reached out and stroked him, there was a slender, green tree-snake.

I guess he must have been a few feet long at least and he was thicker than my arm. He'd just slipped out of his old skin and discarded it further along the branch. I was fascinated. I'd never seen that before. I enjoyed the chattering company of the magpies and the butcher-birds but he was something else. He was the most beautiful creature I'd ever come across.

I said hello. Though I hated being touched I loved to touch new things and new people. I was sorely tempted to reach out to him but I got the distinct impression he didn't want me to. I realised he was a lot like me and I respected that.

His scales were coloured a truly breathtaking emerald green; like sparkling jewels they were. And his eyes were a gorgeous amber exactly like traffic lights, with a slit of black down the middle. He darted his tongue about trying to talk to me.

I asked him if he knew where King Koala lived. The snake approached very slowly looking me straight in the eye all the while. He raised his head a little and arched his back; almost brushing my bare thigh. I saw his mouth open and then, just as he was about to answer me, Mother called out my name. I hated my name. I shivered at the sound of it. I still do.

Green tree-man froze and cautiously withdrew a little. I could hear that Mother was angry but I had to know the answer to my question. I asked him again. He hissed something and puffed up the blue scales under his chin like a balloon. I told him I didn't understand.

Mother wanted to know who I was talking to. I said it was the green tree-man. I thought of him as a man. In my mind he was certainly no different from me. You should've seen her face when she caught sight of that snake stretched out on the branch beside me with his throat puffed up. She was shaking at the knees. I'd never seen her so frightened before. In fact I only saw her that terrified once again. I laughed at her.

All of a sudden she grabbed me by the ankle and dragged me off the branch. I landed hard on the ground with the wind knocked out of me. I was so shocked I couldn't struggle so she easily pulled me through the long grass away from the tree. I was locked in the closet for the rest of the day.

'No supper for you, you stupid boy.'

I suppose she thought that was a harsh punishment but I was glad to be in the closet and I didn't care much about food. That evening I was brought before Father with my head hung low as the story was recounted.

Father simply said I was an idiot. Then he climbed the tree to kill the snake. With tears in my eyes I begged him not to hurt my friend but he didn't listen. He cut the green tree-man up into little pieces with a cane knife and put the bits on a bonfire. He said snakes were dangerous and I mustn't play with them or I'd get bitten.

'You'll get yourself killed,' Father yelled.

I wished I'd been bitten. I've never forgiven myself for my part in the green tree-man's death. After that I was very careful who they caught me speaking to. I never brought friends home.

A few days later I climbed the mango tree and found the discarded translucent snakeskin. I took it back to my room and kept it secret from everyone until I was nineteen years old. The only person I ever told about it was Nanna-Father.

After the incident with the snake I was allowed more time with the telly. Within 12 months, thanks to the miracle of television, my grammar was improving and my vocabulary expanded all the time. This was because during the day I was free to repeat everything I heard on the telly over and over to my heart's content without annoying anyone. I knew to keep quiet in the evening.

I loved mimicking the voices I heard and trying to make sense of what they said. In those days Australian television presenters always affected an educated English accent. That's probably how I ended up sounding so English. I loved the telly. It didn't smack me across the head when I parroted its own words back at it. It told me things – interesting things – about other places and other peoples. It inspired me. I began to make plans to escape Mother's prison.

My life entered a new phase. Every day I talked more and more. I repeated news reports word for word. I mimicked the singers in Mother's record collection with perfect pitch. Nanna loved my imitation of Bing Crosby singing 'Don't Fence Me In'. I'm sure I didn't know the first thing about irony in those days; I just loved that song.

Then I began saying things that offended people. I said what was on my mind. I didn't hold back. I was impolite. I was brutally honest. I was rude.

Mother took me to the barber every fortnight to have my head shaved so I couldn't pull my hair out. One week there was a man in the barber's chair who had no nose, just two long furrows in his face where his nose should have been. I asked him who'd cut off his beak.

Mother was horrified. She slapped me hard in the face and told me to say sorry. As soon as I'd apologised she dragged me outside. She said he was a soldier who'd been a prisoner of war and I shouldn't say such awful things. I wanted to be a soldier. Then everyone would be polite to me.

I said much worse things. If I noticed someone telling a lie, I'd pipe up and point it out. I copped my first taste of the strap for that. Father didn't like being contradicted in front of his elder sister. Children should be seen and not heard. Silence is golden. Speak when you're spoken to.

Nevertheless I copied the colourful expressions Australians are famous for whenever I heard them. Bloody bastard was my first and it's still my personal favourite. I love alliteration. Then came bugger and arsehole. Little turd – I heard that a lot. So how could they expect me not to repeat it? Dickhead was probably the worst thing you could call someone in those days. I addressed everyone I met with it.

'Hello, you bloody dickhead.'

Strangers sniggered behind their hands. Mother blushed deeply and always gave me a good hiding.

When I failed to keep quiet at dinner, in front of guests or in my sleep, food was withheld from me. I didn't care. Food wasn't important. Especially not the tasteless grey mush Mother served up.

When I screamed out for no apparent reason, my parents locked me in the closet and called me an uncontrollable child. I loved that place. Mother called it the closet of remorse. Once the door shut I knew I'd be left alone for hours.

In fact I believe I may have begun a rudimentary practice of meditation in that closet. I had a blanket on the floor, and the section she locked me in was just wide enough so I could comfortably sit cross-legged. I used to put my hands in my lap, shut down all my senses and go off into the world of my imagination – the place I'd later know as the Far Country.

Our local doctor reckoned I was being deliberately difficult just to get attention. He solemnly informed me I was going to be beaten whenever I broke the rules. I told him he was a dickhead and probably a bloody bastard as well.

He advised my mother that if she was going to thrash me, she shouldn't hold back. In the long run it would all be for my own good. He gave her more advice out of my hearing but the basis of it all was pain, pain and more pain. Silly old bugger. That tactic didn't have much chance of success.

I've always had a strange relationship with pain. I experience pain – there's no doubt about it. It's just that I don't usually take much notice of it, unless it's unexpected. Pain is always overwhelming. Anything I find overwhelming I simply shut out completely so it ceases to exist. I suppose I had to learn to shut pain down from an early age. I was beaten so much there was little practical alternative for me.

The violent treatment regularly meted out to me probably has to be understood in the context of the times. Horses were still common in Brisbane in the sixties. When they were not working they had heavy hobbles made of timber strapped around their legs so they couldn't wander too far. Horses were beaten if they didn't obey their masters.

Dogs were also badly treated in those days. Dogs were rarely kept as pets back then. They were working animals. A dog was expected to know its duties, keep its place and do as it was told, especially the last one. Children were considered on a par with dogs or horses. If a dog continued to be disobedient, it was beaten more savagely. If it showed no signs of improvement, it would be shot. That's the only detail that set children apart from dogs.

Pain was as much a part of my day-to-day life as it would have been for any recalcitrant working dog. The only difference was I didn't learn from pain. I simply learned to shut it out. It became little more than a warning signal to me.

I vividly recall the morning Mother brought out a rolling pin for the first time. I can remember thinking this was going to be a completely new experience. I wondered how much it was going to hurt. I sat down in a corner and shivered waiting for the pain to start. The anticipation was always worse than the punishment. However, on this occasion she didn't hit me with it. She held me down and stuck one of the handles deep into my backside.

I think I can honestly say I've never experienced anything so agonising in my life either before or since. I screamed and screamed until I finally managed to get away from her and run for the closet of remorse. I hid in there clinging to a rack on the back of the door so she couldn't open it. I stayed there two days before I ventured out. My pants were caked in blood and I had trouble walking for a week.

That rolling pin did more than just superficial physical damage to me. After that I learned to split into two people. There was me – the little boy who loved adventuring and sitting by himself; then there was the toughened man who could take any punishment dished out to him without showing any sign of pain or distress.

When I quizzed Mother about this incident before her death she told me I hadn't done anything particularly wrong that day. She was just following the doctor's advice. Since beatings hadn't been enough to convince me to change my ways he thought Mother should try something more drastic. The rolling pin was his diabolical idea.

It may have been after that experience that another aspect of my relationship with pain developed. I can't be certain which came first. However, I do remember I hated going to the toilet. I'd hold my shit until I was so badly constipated I'd be doubled up in agony. Sometimes I wouldn't be able to wear shorts or even walk a few steps. For years I only ever emptied my bowels once a week at most. Though it often restricted my movement, I ignored the pain. Anything was better than the toilet.

In the mid-sixties the sewer system hadn't reached the outer suburbs of Brisbane where the farms and the bush began. The outside toilet, nicknamed the dunny can, was a little shed in the back garden. It was just big enough to house a large tin set inside a wooden box that had a hole cut in the top.

In daylight the whole world could see me going out there. I hated being watched so I rarely went by day. I've always been an extremely private person. After sunset there were bad feelings hanging around the dunny. I was afraid of these feelings and I didn't like passing through their encircling barrier.

By the age of six I'd worked out that no one else could sense these bad feelings. By then I'd begun to think of the bad feelings as people. I couldn't see them in a conventional way. I just knew they were there. Mother gave me a terrible beating if I ever mentioned them. She told me over and over how stupid I was to believe in invisible people. I just learned to shut up about them altogether.

There were good people too. They visited me in my room and they sat around under the mango tree in the shade on the hottest days of summer laughing and telling stories. They came from the creek. That was their home. Sometimes, if I went walking down by the trickling water all by myself, they followed me around. They were full of fun and laughter.

I spoke to a psychologist recently who explained that I was severely traumatised as a child. She said these imaginary people were probably by-products of physical trauma.

After the rolling pin I used to go off into a trance a lot more than I had before. I called it going away. As I grew older I referred to the trance state as the Far Country. Everything else was the Near Country, including my nightmares. I was going away in my head because the physical abuse was just too much to bear.

The Far Country was a land of enchantment where I could meet interesting people, sing songs, hear stories and relax. It was like Heaven without all the hymns. The Near Country, on the other hand, was a painful Hell inhabited by vicious, cruel, unfeeling demonic entities who, perversely, loved to sing hymns. The human mind is a fascinating mechanism. We have it built in to us to survive the most horrendous events by tapping into the well of our imagination.

Whether my good people existed or not doesn't much matter to me now. I went through a period in my fifth year when I sneaked out at every opportunity to bathe in their presence. Mother had to watch me like a hawk. One morning I ran off into the bush with a vague plan to follow the trickling waters of the creek down to the Brisbane River. I knew it led to the ocean. I thought I'd build myself a raft and row to Fiji.

I didn't get far before the prickly lantana bushes completely enclosed the banks. They were so thick I couldn't go any further along the creek. By then Mother had discovered I was missing.

I sat terrified on the sandy bank for ages while she ran around screaming out my name. When I heard her threatening to thrash me I crawled
deep into the very heart of the lantana bushes. I cut my hands, face and
bare feet on the thorny spikes. There was blood all over me. The pain was
easier to deal with than Mother's wrath, so I stayed put.

After a long while she gave up yelling out for me. I relaxed and fell
asleep in my spiky bed. When I woke up there was a man with a black face
squatting on the creek bank. He was looking straight at me. His skin was
so black it looked almost blue. He wore a dusty, tattered, old brown
suit-coat and trousers. His feet were bare.

I'd never seen an Aboriginal Australian up that close before. They had
a big camp in the city in Musgrave Park that we'd passed on our way to
visit Nanna and Pop. I'd seen groups of them sitting under the trees or
around their cooking fires. Nanna called them blackfellas.

The blackfella smiled at me through his bushy beard as he drew
something in the sand with his finger. Then he was laughing but he
wasn't laughing at me like Pop did. He was laughing for joy. He seemed
so gentle. So I crawled out to get a closer look. I let him take me by the
hand and without a word he led me along the creek toward home.

When we got to the mango tree he nimbly climbed up into the
branches and then he was stuffing his pockets with the ripe fruit. I tried to
follow him but he wouldn't let me near. I thought he was angry with me.
Suddenly I felt terribly guilty. I told him it was my fault the green
tree-man got chopped up and thrown on the bonfire. The blackfella
laughed, showing me his beautiful white teeth.

Then Mother appeared.

'Who are you talking to, you bloody idiot?'

She grabbed me by the scruff of the neck and dragged me back to the
house.

'Blackfella,' was all I managed to say.

I grabbed her skirts and begged Mother not to kill him.

'What blackfella?'

I turned to look back at the tree. I could just make out two sparkling
eyes peeping out from between the leaves higher up in the branches.
Mother squinted as she followed my line of sight but she didn't see him.

'They should've drowned you at birth. If you're going to run away
why can't you do a bloody good job of it?'

Mother slapped me to the ground, then she dragged me upstairs by the ankles and scrubbed me with a hard brush until my skin was red raw. She rubbed iodine into my cuts and put me to bed without any supper. When I looked out the window the blackfella was gone and so were most of the mangoes. I was very upset. I wished I'd thought to ask him where King Koala lived.

When Father got home that evening I got a hiding. He told me he'd put me in a mental home if I ran off like that again. 'What do you think you're doing making up stories about blackfellas? You scared the wits out of your mother.'

'*He's* a bloody blackfella,' Mother mocked.

The nickname stuck for a long while. The whole family called me blackfella. Shortly after that I met my great-grandmother for the first time.

'Where's the little blackfella?' she laughed and the room was full of sniggering taunts. I called her a bloody bastard. That was the last time I was allowed to see my great-grandmother. She passed away not long after.

Father's warnings didn't stop me running away every few weeks. I was beginning to see that Father didn't command much respect from anyone. I heard Mother calling him all sorts of names behind his back. If I cried for any reason, she used to say, 'I should have known you'd turn out like your old man.'

I was still in awe of him at that stage. When he said I was headstrong, I took careful note. He called me wilful. He reckoned I was too wild. Why couldn't I just be calm, compliant and normal like everyone else? Another time he sat me down and warned me I'd have to pull up my socks or there'd be trouble – big trouble.

By then I was generally getting more and more agitated. When I sat on my chair by the window I'd be tapping my heel on the floor and drumming my fingers. I'd fly into terrible rages if my concentration was interrupted. The rages were truly awful. I'd have the strength of ten men and I could do as much damage as twenty. I threw chairs about. I ripped books in half. I hated books because Mother used to hit me with them. I'd grab them off her and toss them at the windows. She told me that in my early years I used to punch and kick her but she soon put a stop to that.

Mother worked out the best way to deal with my violence was to pick me up and slam me into a wall to knock the wind out of me. If I still had any fight left in me, she'd lay into me with a strap until I'd managed to crawl away out of its reach under a bed or table to catch my breath. I'd fall asleep there after a beating or in the closet of remorse.

Mother told me years later that she had often been tempted to break my neck and end her misery. 'What did I do to deserve you?' she spat at me a few months before she passed away. 'I wish I'd let the doctors put you down,' she added. 'It would've been best for everyone.'

This may be obvious to you, but I've only just begun to realise that at the time I was just a frightened little autistic boy. It has been a great revelation for me to discover it wasn't my fault that I suffered the rages or misbehaved. I didn't really understand what was expected of me. I was absolutely lost. Everything was so overwhelming.

The rages became worse so, not surprisingly, as Father had promised, there was trouble. Truckloads of it.

One day Mother lost her temper with me. I can only vaguely remember this incident perhaps because it was so much worse than anything I'd experienced before. Years later, before she died, Mother explained she'd done it all for my own good. She laughed fondly at the memory as she revealed to me the details. She reckoned she was just trying to knock some sense into me, whatever that means. Mother insisted none of it was her fault.

'You can't blame me,' she said. 'I was at the end of my tether. You were a little bastard.'

I don't recall what sparked it all off. Neither did she. The first thing she remembered she was screaming at me that I'd ruined her life. She scared me so much I spontaneously released the putrid, compacted contents of my bowels. We were in her immaculately clean kitchen at the time. I suppose that must have been what pushed her over the edge.

She picked me up by the scruff and shrieked at me – calling me a filthy bastard. 'You're a bloody animal!' she yelled. 'You dirty little black-fella!' As she held me up by the collar she asked God why He'd dumped me in her lap. What had she done to deserve it? Why couldn't she have had a normal little boy instead of a retarded idiot who couldn't even be potty trained?

She threw me against the wall and punched me hard in the face over and over. Apparently I didn't cry. I just put up my hands over my face and curled up tight, as usual, to wait until she was done. When she got tired of punching me, she started kicking. Mother shouted she was going to hand me over to the police if I didn't change my ways.

'What makes you like this? You should be bloody ashamed of yourself.' Next thing she had a wooden spoon and she was laying into my head, arms, legs and any piece of exposed flesh with it.

'Say sorry!' she screamed over and over, but I still couldn't make a sound. I must have been frozen with fear.

She reckoned I eventually managed to promise I was sorry and that I'd never do it again, though I'm sure I'd already forgotten whatever it was that had set her off on the tirade.

I had excrement all over me. It was smeared on my arms and my cheeks. All of a sudden she calmed down. She picked me up by the scruff of the neck and dragged me into the bathroom. I cowered in the corner while she ran the bath.

I endured terrible nightmares about this incident on and off for most of my life. The nightmares didn't stop until after I saw Mother's corpse lying cold and lifeless in her hospital bed.

My dreams have confused the whole episode in my memory so I can't recall all the details of what she did to me. But, from what she told me, I must have known I was in real trouble. It was always worse whenever Mother went quiet. In the nightmare I'm so desperately frightened I can't straighten my legs to stand up and run away.

Mother grabbed me again.

'You should've been drowned at birth and saved us all the bother.'

She put my head under water and held me there. I struggled desperately to begin with but she was so much stronger than me. It was stupid to fight her. She always won. Before long I gave up and let my body relax.

It was probably lucky that I did. My response shocked her. She pulled me out of the bath, slapped my face until I coughed up all the water then threw a towel at me and ran outside crying.

When Father came home that evening the mess had been cleaned up. I was locked in my room – nothing unusual there – and Mother said nothing about what had happened. She never spoke of it again until years later when she was dying of cancer. It had been her intention to drown me, but when I went limp she realised there'd be consequences for her actions.

She said, 'If I'd been put in gaol for murder there would've been no one left to look after your sister.'

I'd already been trying to stay a step ahead of Mother for a good while. For example, I'd got into the habit of stealing her rolling pins. She must have bought 30 of them over a period of five years. Inside a wall under the house there was an empty space that could only be reached through a gap too big for any adult to access. That became the new home for all those frightening weapons of anal intrusion.

After the bathtub I was more scared of Mother than ever before. I was always careful to keep out of her way if I could. The only times I ever let her touch me again was when she hit me. I never really felt comfortable with being touched anyway, but after that the gap between us widened. Mother hardly ever spoke to me again, except in reprimand.

I wasn't being deliberately difficult. As a child I really wanted to please my parents. I'd always try to do as Mother asked but she wasn't very patient with me when I made mistakes or if I didn't clearly understand what she wanted me to do.

Whenever I got a beating she'd yell, 'That's it! I'm calling the police. They're going to take you away to Goodna.' Goodna was the state lunatic asylum. Mother told me that's where uncontrollable children were sent. She used to describe in great detail how I'd be tied up in a room with thick glass windows so I'd always have someone watching me.

She told me I'd be crowded in by all the other lunatics. I'd be strapped to my bed day and night. I'd be force-fed with a tube down my throat. I used to break into a shit-scared shiver whenever she talked about it.

There's nothing that frightens me as much as being touched and being powerless to do anything about it, except being trapped in a room with strangers. The images I had of Goodna absolutely terrified me. Later, Mother revealed to me that it gave her great satisfaction to see me suffering from fear. She felt I deserved it.

I still have nightmares about Goodna, even though I've never been there and it's been renamed and refurbished. I have a powerful imagination. Goodna will always haunt my darkest nightmares.

By the age of six I was being bruised, slapped, kicked and bashed whenever I stepped out of line. Over a period of time blows from her hands and fists gradually affected me less and less. It riled her up that I didn't seem to react when she'd deliver her best punch, so Mother took up a wooden spoon.

She knew it struck terror into my heart. It reminded me of the broad-bladed cane-knife Father had used to kill the green tree-man and the end of the rolling pin at the same time. Every time she picked it up I thought she was going to chop me into bits or stick it up my arse as far as it would go. Mercifully, all she ever did was hit me with it; so things weren't as bad as they might have been.

The wooden spoon worked well until one day she broke it over the back of my head. Then she stepped up to a leather strap. I honestly preferred the strap. It stung a lot more, especially when she turned the buckle end on me, but I was much less frightened of it. If she went for a wooden spoon I'd beg her to use the strap.

Sometimes she punched and kicked me when I was cowering down. Now and then she'd lose all self-control and let fly her pent-up frustration, laying into me until she was too exhausted to stand up. More than once she knocked out a tooth. One day she snapped a big dressmaker's ruler over my head then cursed me for ruining her tools.

This shocks some people when I tell them, but I honestly don't blame Mother for the way she physically mistreated me. I never have. I was shut down during her attacks. I'd switch off all pain. So most of what she did hardly mattered to me. It didn't really touch me at all.

I know I was an awful handful. I used to descend into the most destructive and terrible rages. I ate my own faeces. I spat in the dinner she put down in front of me. I deliberately cut myself open because I was fascinated with blood. I stuck my hand in boiling water on the stove to see what the sensation of scalding was like. I climbed up on the roof and lifted the ceramic tiles to see what was under them. I jumped off the balcony time and again trying to fly. It's a wonder I didn't break my bloody neck.

I sat outside after sunset and talked to the possums in their clicking, squeaky language. I stole leftovers to feed to them. I had to investigate everything and take things apart to see how they worked. And by the age of six I still couldn't go to the toilet properly.

If I was ordered to do something that interfered with my train of thought, I'd simply ignore the interruption. If pressed I might just as easily explode with blinding anger or lapse into a deep trance state where no one could get any response out of me. Sometimes I'd wander in the Far Country for hours; sometimes days. Catatonic was one of Mother's nicknames for me.

Often I'd simply scream for no apparent reason. It was as if a kind of warning siren went off within me when I was overloaded. I wasn't intentionally trying to be difficult. I wasn't being manipulative. But that's how Mother interpreted my behaviour.

In our very last conversation, just before she died, she told me she'd been so desperate to get rid of me she'd left me in a Catholic orphanage. But even the nuns refused to take me.

Apparently no one noticed any significant signs of intelligence in me until just before I started school at six years of age. I didn't want to go. I knew there were other children at school and I didn't want to be around other children. I didn't want to have my world interrupted. I didn't want to socialise or be forced to be somewhere I wasn't familiar with. However, Mother was eager to get rid of me for six hours a day.

In the weeks leading up to my first day, whenever school was mentioned I'd begin screaming. I'd throw things around – chairs, crockery, pots, pans – anything I could get my hands on. I'd bite myself on the arm until I drew blood. I'd tear at my own ears because I had no hair to grab hold of.

I slammed a door into the wall and left a hole in the fibro where the handle struck it. They never let me live that down. That hole was still there when I was 18 and was used to illustrate the fact that I had always been uncontrollably insane.

My behaviour became more and more extreme as school day approached. I ripped my clothes off and ran into the creek naked.

Whenever we were out in public I might suddenly get undressed or wet myself or tear up the bus tickets when the conductor gave them to me. I took to screaming at all hours of the day and night. I didn't understand I was doing the wrong thing. I suppose that reinforced for my family that I wasn't very smart.

Mother dragged me along to another doctor who confirmed that I was an attention seeker. Since punishment hadn't been much of an inducement, he advised her to buy my loyalty. Mother knew I loved music so she bought me a toy violin made of tin. It was a blatant bribe. My parents went on and on about how expensive it was. It cost five dollars.

I felt ashamed that they'd bought me such an extravagant gift. I'd never received anything beautiful from them. I loved that violin and I hated it. I hated that I felt obliged to go to school in return for it. In the end the guilt of the violin convinced me to go.

I don't believe I should ever have been sent to school. The first day I stood at the front fence staring out at the passing traffic on the busy road. I went to the Far Country and no one noticed me until lunch-time. I was put in a class and seated at the back. After an hour or so I ran out and crouched in a corner of the school yard shivering with fear. The teacher had to come and find me.

Next day was the same. I was found at morning tea standing by the front gate. Once again I was taken to class. At lunch-time I ran out into the yard and cowered in a corner. If any children came close, I bellowed like King Koala to scare them off. It worked. No one came near me. When the bell rang I stayed put. I didn't know what it meant. I roared at my teacher, but she was very patient with me and eventually enticed me back to class with a sweet.

The other kids all reckoned I was mad. My cousin was there and he told everyone I was an idiot. It was a short step from there to being called dickhead. That's the name that stuck for the rest of my school life.

I started getting very bad nightmares. Panda bears chopping up snakes with wooden spoons or forcing my head under water; that sort of thing. I slipped into a pattern of staying awake as long as I could at night, lying on my back with my arms stiff by my sides listening intently in case the bad people came into my room.

The mosquito net over my bed was a great comfort. It restricted my vision of the immediate surroundings. I felt like the mosquito net was a shield that protected me from the bad people. The bad people couldn't see through the net. The other great thing about the net was that I could see pictures in the patterns of the weave.

The pictures were like a doorway into my own private world of the imagination. The mosquito net led me into the Far Country where I would sometimes spend the night frolicking with folks who took good care of me. There was wonderful food in the Far Country. There were apples and peaches. There was fresh bread steaming from the oven. And there was fresh cream and honey to eat.

No one grew old in the Far Country and there was no sickness or fighting. No one ever so much as raised their voice in that place except in song. And the wondrous music was utterly captivating. Sometimes I'd go there and imagine myself dancing and dancing until my feet ached and my knees were shaking.

When I think about it now, I understand that my Far Country was no different from the Celtic Otherworld known as the Kingdom of Peace or the Island of the Ever-Young or the Faerie Realm. And to this day I still sleep with a mosquito net draped above the bed, even though there are no mosquitos in the mountains where I live.

The windows of my bedroom always had to be shut, no matter how hot the night, otherwise I couldn't calm down enough to rest. The books on the shelf had to be in their proper positions. Every evening I'd inspect them and take careful note of their positions. In the morning I'd check to see if they'd been disturbed.

The Venetian blinds had to be raised so I could see out into the night. The blinds were only shut when the electric light was on so no one could see into my room. If Mother dusted or rearranged the room while I was at school, I'd become extremely frantic.

Even now I can end up distraught if my wife moves something without telling me. It may take me weeks or even months to notice the disruption, but it sends me into a terrible panic when I do. Sometimes my response involves anxiety and sometimes anger at the interference. It's probably made worse because I've lived most of my adult life completely alone.

The door to my bedroom was a big problem for a long time. I couldn't cope with it being closed at night, but on the other hand, when it was open I could hear the house creaking and every sound in all the other rooms. So I couldn't sleep for the distraction. My sense of hearing has always been acute.

For the first month of school I was sleepwalking almost every night. Eventually Father began locking me in my bedroom. That stopped me wandering the house but caused another problem. I was terrified by Mother's exaggerated stories about the lunatic asylum. Imprisonment in my room caused me unbearable anxiety. The memory of being locked up is still awfully distressing.

I tried tapping my feet. I tried shaking my hands. I tried pacing the room. I knocked my forehead against the wall; but nothing could get me to sleep. With the door shut I could never hope to calm down. I was forced to sit at the window until I was too exhausted to keep my eyes open.

If my room hadn't been above a large privet hedge I would've jumped out the window and run away. Many times I'd leapt off the balcony on to the grass but I couldn't bring myself to land in that hedge. It was too neatly trimmed. It's just as well. I probably would have killed myself.

I hardly ever closed my eyes until after the sun came up. I stayed in bed long after the rest of the household stirred. I'd get a beating for that. At school I'd fall asleep in class.

I was undernourished and exhausted. I stank because I was always constipated. I sweated toxins in the tropical heat. I suffered terrible earaches for days on end, but I wouldn't dare say anything about it in case I got into more trouble. Mother was always telling me I was a whining little bastard.

I didn't want to be a little bastard but it seemed I just couldn't help myself. Soon I was under enormous pressure to behave like everyone else. I was beginning to crack. I'd take off my clothes in class when I got over-heated. My teacher learned to keep an eye out for the first sign of that.

Sometimes my bowels would simply release their contents without warning. That happened once in the playground and another time on a visit to relatives. I was spending longer and longer periods away from the toilet. Within a few months a stranger just had to look at me to spark off a fit of screaming.

Then one night as I was drifting off into my own world sitting on my chair at the window a terrifying thing happened. My worst fears became reality. Without warning, a wild face suddenly appeared. It had huge black eyes surrounded with circles of grey-brown. There were yellow fangs and a purple tongue protruding from black lips. Two tiny black hands pressed against the glass.

If I saw that face today, I'd instantly recognise it as a ring-tail possum. I should've recognised it back then but I was very jumpy. I was so startled I fell backwards on to the mosquito net, bringing the whole lot down and making an awful noise. The possum didn't hang about.

I heard Father cursing as he got up to see what was the trouble. He struggled with the lock on my door, getting more and more angry as he fumbled about trying to reach me. By the time he got into my room he was so enraged he just looked at the great tear in the net and exploded. He picked up the tin violin and started clubbing me with it. I didn't cower.

I recall feeling as if I was watching the whole episode from outside myself. It was a strange experience. I saw myself slump over with blood all over my face. Mother came into the room. I heard her talking, but her voice sounded as if she had a blanket over her mouth. She didn't seem at all upset about what she saw. Father bundled me into the car and drove me away.

The next thing I remember I was in a room at the children's hospital where I was born. A doctor was changing the dressings on my head-wounds. I had a dozen stitches, and I bear a scar over my eye to this day where one of the blows almost took my left eyebrow clean off. Every time I look in the mirror I remember Father.

No one ever asked me how I came to be so badly cut and bruised about the face. Father told them I fell off my bicycle. He never had any trouble lying if the occasion called for it. I guess that's where I learned to do it.

The trouble with his story was that I didn't have a bicycle and it was the middle of the night. The nurse grudgingly accepted his explanation though I could see she was sceptical. It was the sixties. Adults didn't ask children questions in those days and no one challenged a parent's right to punish their offspring as they saw fit.

I was kept out of school for a fortnight. So I suppose it was worth it. I got a new mosquito net too. My old one was torn and covered in blood. The new one didn't have any holes. It felt like Christmas. The new net had all sorts of wonderful pictures in its storybook weave.

The face of the bad person-possum and many others like him visited me at the window almost every night after that. They unsettled me a lot. I'd just huddle under the sheet and shake.

My new net eventually helped me calm down. It was a magical barrier against evil. I soon became quite comfortable with the routine of the bad person's visits. In time I actually looked forward to him dropping by. I told my teacher about the bad person. She was the only adult I trusted. She laughed.

That laugh wasn't the only thing about my teacher that reminded me of the blackfella. She was gentle. She liked to take me by the hand and I let her. She never hit me when I did the wrong thing. She never raised her voice. I was fiercely loyal to her. I wanted to please her so much that I stopped shouting in class. I literally bit my tongue when I was tempted to scream out. I tried going to the school toilet.

She told me she'd help me to be a good boy. She told me she was sure there was a good boy inside me. She tried putting her arm around me and I allowed her because I didn't want to be a bad boy. I didn't want to go to the lunatic asylum. I knew if I didn't behave I'd be locked up.

My teacher arranged it so that I'd be in her class for my first three years of school. She was so very kind to me that I gradually came to accept and enjoy being at school. She never forced me to do anything I didn't want to. When the other children were doing maths I'd be allowed to practise writing in chalk on a little slate.

I wasn't being beaten up as much by Mother either because I was away from home all day. However, I was becoming more and more confused. I couldn't tell one day from another; they all sort of melted into each other. It seemed like I was always either surrounded by the unbearable noise of school or seated by my window alone in the night with only flickering breaks of television in between.

When swimming season came around I refused to go into the pool. I retreated from the stench of the big expanse of chlorinated water. I simply couldn't stand the awful smell. I ran out the school gate in my bathing shorts and kept running until a police car stopped me.

I was taken back to school, but on the way I called the policeman a bastard. He gave me a good hiding with his belt before he took me to the principal. Mother was called and she gave me another terrible beating in front of my teacher. I was red and bruised all over. As usual I didn't cry.

My teacher was much nicer to me after that. I was allowed to sit by the pool and watch the others taking swimming lessons. My teacher said I could join in whenever I wanted to. So every week I'd take my towel and swimming shorts along to school but I never went into the change rooms. I never went swimming.

Shortly after that Mother took me to see a psychologist. I won't easily forget him. He was the first American I ever met. He was impossibly tall and gangly. I asked him if he was a stick insect. Mother slapped me.

He sternly insisted she leave the room. I was surprised when she meekly obeyed him. I liked the Stick-Insect. As soon as Mother was gone he threw a basketball at me. I'd never seen a basketball. No one had ever thrown any kind of ball to me. It hit me in the chest, knocked me over, then it rolled away. I didn't make a sound. I just sat there on the floor staring at him wondering what I'd done wrong.

He retrieved the ball and told me to try catching it. I got up. He threw it again. It hit me in the chest and bounced off but it didn't knock me over this time. I was ready for it. He laughed at me and told me I was doing fine.

'But could you try to catch the ball with your hands?'

'You're American,' I ventured.

'Yes, I am.'

'Do they have stick insects in America?'

'Of course.'

'Are you on television?'

That was the only place I'd ever heard an American accent before.

'No.'

'I'm sorry,' I said.

The Stick-Insect was laughing again as he threw the ball. This time I caught it in my hands though it stung my palms and threw me off balance. I had to step back. I stood for a few moments proudly holding the ball at chest height while he waited for my next move.

'Are you going to throw it back to me?'

The American laughed like my teacher.

'I'm sorry,' I stuttered.

Before long we were passing the ball back and forth as I answered his questions. He asked me what my favourite television show was. At the time I was a huge fan of the classic science fiction series from Britain, Doctor Who. To prove it I perfectly mimicked one of the Daleks; the race of evil machine creatures who are the Doctor's greatest enemies.

Offering my best Dalek impersonation I said, 'So Doctor, we meet at last... Exterminate!'

A Dalek has a very distinctive machine-like voice that's very difficult for most people to imitate. I'd been doing Daleks for a long while. It's still a bit of a party trick for me. My Dalek voice has come in very handy for fending off unwanted attention; it usually confirms my madness. The psychologist wasn't smiling or laughing any more. He looked shocked.

'I'm sorry,' I offered. I was very concerned that I'd gone too far.

'What are you sorry for?'

'Doing the wrong thing.'

'Do you think you've done the wrong thing?'

'Yes. I'm stupid.'

'Do you think you're stupid?'

'Yes.'

He frowned as he put out his hand toward my shoulder but I retreated out of his reach to the corner of the room. I expected he was going to slap me. I curled up waiting for a hiding. The American summoned Mother back into his office.

When she returned, he told her there wasn't any place for me in the mental home. There were too many others waiting who were worse off than me. I was put back to the bottom of the list while more tests were arranged. I was so happy I smiled broadly like a gormless idiot.

Mother cried and begged him to take me.

'Look at him,' she sobbed. 'He's brainless.'

She told him I'd taken to punching my sister. I called her a bloody liar. She was. Mother strode over to the corner and slapped me with the back of her hand.

'Say sorry!' she yelled.

'I'm sorry.'

The Stick-Insect grabbed her hand and told her to stop. He advised her she'd have to put up with me a bit longer. He wrote out some instructions and gave her a brown bottle.

I took three of his pills every day; morning, noon and night. I don't know what the pills were but they changed my life profoundly. I slept all night and I hardly had the energy to utter a sound all day long. I don't remember much of my waking life for the rest of that year.

The nightmares tapered off. Up to then I'd equated my nightmares with the real world, what I called the Near Country. Once I started taking the pills my dreams became very vivid and they didn't seem to end when I got up in the morning. The Far Country was everywhere. The Near receded.

The border between dream and reality that had been fairly distinct before my visit to the Stick-Insect was gradually becoming more and more blurred. I didn't drift off into trances any more. I was in a permanent trance.

As soon as the other school children realised I'd lost the will to bellow at them, the bullying and the beatings began in earnest. I didn't have the strength or the will to fight back.

By the end of grade one I hadn't learned to write. I could spell simple words. I could read out loud and sound exactly like a television newsreader, but I couldn't tell my teacher what the story I was reading was all about. I could count to one thousand but I couldn't make sense of addition, multiplication or subtraction. I spent a lot of time with my friend the telly. I was off in the Far Country.

At the end of the year my teacher told the class she was getting married. I saw how happy she was and I was surprised. My parents were married and they weren't happy. No one I knew was married *and* happy. The next year she taught for a few months before she left on maternity leave.

I was placed in a new class with a teacher who was the complete opposite of my first one. For a start she was hugely fat. In those days over-weight people were very unusual. The other thing that was strange about her was that she rarely smiled.

The other children sniggered at her name. I don't recall what it was. It might have been Miss Bullcock or something equally amusing to the crude humour of a tittering seven-year-old. I couldn't bring myself to say it. I hated names. Whenever she strode into the room I'd say 'Good morning' with everyone else. Then I'd mime her name. She never noticed. I knew her as Fat Lady. It was a title not a name.

The very moment I first walked into her class she told me I'd been mollycoddled and that I wouldn't have it so easy in future. I was lazy and bad and she wouldn't let me get away with it.

'What you need is a firm hand, my lad.'

The first day I stood in the corner with the idiot-hat on so I'd know what it felt like. That ended up being a daily ritual. I didn't mind. My legs would go numb while I was standing in the corner, but she never asked me any questions and nothing was expected of me. Perhaps Stick-Insect's pills took the edge off the experience. I suppose she used me as a kind of comic relief to keep the other children in line.

However, her idea of discipline didn't begin or end with ridicule. Within a month she'd hit me with rulers, fists, the back of her hand and a heavy wooden compass meant for scribing chalk circles on the black-board.

I was moved to the back of the class. I was kept in at morning tea and lunch. Not that I cared. I wasn't all that fussed about food. I could take it or leave it. And as long as I was in the classroom the other kids couldn't beat me up. I could go off to the Far Country.

Around that time I pretty much stopped talking altogether. Eventually I was being sent to the principal once a week for the cuts. 'The cuts' was what we called a caning across the palm of the hand. The worse your crime, the thinner the strip of cane. If you were really bad you got it across the back of the hand. That left your knuckles bruised. I still have scars on the backs of my hands where the splintering cane took out little nicks of skin.

Fat Lady delighted in sending me to the office on cold winter mornings. When I'd get back she'd ask me if my hands were stinging. All my classmates used to laugh. It was the only time I ever saw Fat Lady smile. I never answered her.

Eventually the principal got to know me. He must have realised there was something wrong. I didn't even flinch when he caned me. He'd read me the note from Fat Lady — 'This impudent lad should receive six of the best please.' Then he'd sit me down in his office and try to get me to talk.

He gave up on that after a few weeks. One day he advised me to hold my hand tightly when I walked into class and pretend I was in pain.

'Don't worry. I won't cane you again. When you're sent up here just wait outside my office for a while then go back to class. It'll be our little secret.'

Then he patted me on the head and told me not to annoy my teacher so much. After that I didn't bother going to the office. I'd stand at the front fence as I'd done on my first day. I liked counting cars. Soon I was classifying them according to make, year and model. I'd stand there until at least 20 Fords had passed by. I couldn't leave until that had happened.

By that stage I was being bullied every day. I had a permanent nose bleed and my ears were in constant pain from being bashed. I started getting awful headaches that made me throw up. No one ever asked me how I was feeling. I thought I wasn't allowed to say anything. My nose still bleeds to this day. It was broken around that time either by Mother or some petty playground bully. I suspect that the Stick-Insect's pills may have been a greater comfort to me than I could know.

My life went on in a blur of beatings and bullying until one evening a terrible shock hit the family. Father came home early from work. He was very upset. He'd lost his job and he was bitterly ashamed.

He'd been about to be promoted to warehouse manager but he'd been caught helping to steal a case of whiskey. His boss had sacked him on the spot without any pay. He was lucky the police weren't called in.

Mother yelled and threw crockery at him. I crept out to the kitchen door and glimpsed him seated at the table with tears running down his face. He was drinking overproof rum and chain-smoking cheap cigarettes. When he saw me he bluntly suggested that I might like to fuck off.

I stayed away from both of them. Later that evening I heard Mother explaining the situation to Nanna on the telephone. Belts were going to have to be tightened, she said. It was going to be hard for Father to find another job without a reference.

Nanna promised to help out financially. Later she told me I'd have to be the man of the house now that Father had shown his true colours. No one had ever spoken to me like that before. I decided I'd do my best to help out. The only other men I knew were Uncle, who had the chicken farm, and Pop. They became my role models.

The pills soon ran out and there was no money to buy more. When they were gone I stopped sleeping through the night, but ever since that time my dreams have run into my waking life. I still classify nightmares as belonging to the real world, the Near Country. Dreams and trances belong to the Far Country.

The end of the pills also meant I had a lot more energy. After school I'd go over to Uncle's farm and follow him around hoping to learn something. He had a broad Glasgow accent, which I easily copied. He was like Pop in some ways. They were around the same age and they were strong, able men.

I'm sure Uncle didn't know what to make of me. He probably suspected I was perpetually mocking him. Most of what passed for humour in Queensland in those days was based on cruel mockery, mindless goading or petulant derision; especially when it was directed toward outsiders. And I was certainly considered an outsider.

My cousin used to bash me and tell me to go home. His old man would watch me getting beaten up. Sometimes he'd shake his head when I fell to the ground. He'd always walk away, unwilling to intervene.

I took a few weeks of this punishment before Auntie told me not to come and visit. My cousin also got a talking to from his mother. I don't think he ever forgave me for whatever trouble I got him into.

Forced to observe from a distance I watched Uncle working. I'd take note of every detail. I was there when he fed the chickens, turned eggs in the incubator, cut chaff for the goat or ploughed the soil behind an antique rotary hoe that spewed black diesel-smoke as the engine cranked up.

He and his son played some pretty nasty tricks on me, but I stuck it out and eventually I was allowed to cut wood for the cooking fire and help shovel out the chicken sheds. When Mother found out how I was spending my afternoons she put an abrupt end to it. My hopes of becoming the man of the house were dashed.

Around that time that I started talking to myself, a habit that persists. Nowadays I have it mostly under control and only indulge when I know I'm alone. It goes without saying this habit made my life in the playground much worse.

I don't recall the details of how it happened, but one day I was being pushed around by some big bully from the upper grades. I was trying to ignore him but somehow my rage just boiled over. I punched this boy hard in the nose and knocked him flat.

Things turned around pretty quickly after that. By the time the summer holidays began the other kids were much more wary of me. The bullying had stopped altogether and things quietened down. All those trips to the principal for the cane had earned me a strange kind of respect. I was sorry school had to end for six weeks. I didn't want to have to spend all summer with my family.

I survived that year having learned one very valuable lesson. If I played dumb no one expected too much from me. Over the previous few months, for the lack of any other man to look up to, Pop had become my role model.

I noticed how much respect everyone showed him. I didn't understand the respect was based on fear. Whenever we visited my grandparents I'd observe him closely. I took to wearing a battered old Stetson hat just like his.

I got hold of my first waistcoat, one of Pop's cast-offs. Mother didn't like me wearing that so I kept it in my closet and only put it on when I was alone. I mimicked his laconic, self-deprecating sense of humour. I stole some tobacco and cigarette papers from Father and learned to roll a cigarette with one hand. I never smoked them. That wasn't the point.

At home I was becoming more and more violent. I stood up to Mother for the first time as I'd stood up to the fourth-grade bully. Whenever she hit me, I'd hit her back exactly the same way. When she told me to do something I'd tell her to go do it herself – you bloody bastard.

Of course, I was never going to get the edge on Mother. She wasn't a petty schoolyard bully. She was a full-grown, life-size bully with a leather strap and an impressive array of wooden weapons at her disposal with which to knock the living daylights out of me.

Let's not forget the rolling pin either. When she realised it was me stealing her rolling pins she bought a new one. She got in the habit of putting it in a different place after every session. All she had to do was bring it out and I'd just about wet myself with fear. Mother was a tough-nut and, as she often said, no skinny retard was going to push her around.

I don't know where I would have ended up if things had gone on like that. I probably would've run away from home and eventually found myself in a penal home for boys or the lunatic asylum. But it didn't turn out that way.

School ended for the summer holidays and within a week my life was turned upside down. The unexpected events of that summer proved to be devastating for my family but if things hadn't turned out that way I don't imagine I'd be alive to tell you about it.

Three

A single word is all it takes to change a life.
A single word uttered with passion
Can demolish or renovate the house of the heart.
Every syllable has the potential for transforming
Dreams into reality and nightmares into flesh.
Whether you choose to speak with malice or with Love
Is entirely up to you.

In my eighth year I was constantly being told I was stupid, fat-headed, contrary and foul-tempered. Father used to say if I was a dog I'd have been drowned long ago. I don't believe he ever found out how close Mother came to making that a reality.

When I first heard the word autistic I didn't have a clue what it meant. We'd visited the Stick-Insect a few times and I'd been given various written tests to perform. The last time I saw him was also the last week of second grade. I was left alone in the waiting room while he spoke with Mother.

On the bus home she didn't say a word. I thought to myself, this is the calm before the storm. I was understandably apprehensive. Usually she couldn't resist chastising me for more than half an hour at a time. I hated it when she saved up all her anger.

I began to shut down preparing for the battering to come. However, it was one of those rare occasions when the storm seemed to blow over. The pressure continued to build up to a frightening intensity.

On the first morning of summer holidays I stepped out of line as usual and Mother dished out a particularly awful beating. After I'd begged forgiveness on my knees I was locked in the closet of remorse. I sat there, cross-legged, rubbing my thighs where she'd caught me with the strap. I was ordered to say 'I'm sorry' a thousand times.

There I was reciting my penance when I overheard Mother talking to Nanna on the phone. Amongst all the terrible things Mother said about me, in between the curses and the bitterness, I was sure she said I was *artistic*. That took me completely by surprise because I'd never heard her say anything good about me before. By then I was convinced she despised me.

I was very confused. I understood that artistic wasn't a bad thing. My first teacher often said I was very artistic. I hurried through my 'sorrys' with a light heart. I was feeling unimaginably better about myself. I wanted Mother to love me and to be proud of me, as any little boy does.

A switch flicked on inside me. I emerged from shut-down so I could set about living up to the label she'd given me. I decided I was going to be an artist. And you can rest assured, when I decide to do something, there's absolutely no stopping me.

How's that for irony? I probably never would have picked up a paintbrush or a pencil if I hadn't heard her reporting to Nanna what the Stick-Insect had said about me.

I knew that artists were respected. As I sat cross-legged in the closet I realised there was some hope for me. I didn't have to continue to be the little bastard. I could make something of my life if I put some effort into learning a craft.

A long while passed during which time I continued to believe she'd used the word artistic. I took up drawing and painting on the strength of that silly misunderstanding, so typical of the problems I had with interpreting the world when I was a child.

Four years later when I discovered that autistic wasn't a very pleasant thing to be called, I wasn't particularly surprised. By then I'd come to understand Mother would always hold me in deep contempt. But I already considered myself to be an artist and I didn't really care what she called me behind my back any more.

I can look back on that time fairly objectively now. I recognise that the first split in my identity was probably still a narrow crack. Cracking up was a survival mechanism. When you consider the pressure I was under it's obvious something had to give.

From the sanctuary of my dark, cramped closet I planned my new self very carefully. In order to become an artist I had to learn a new set of skills. That wasn't going to be a difficulty for me; any outcome I focus on is within my reach. The only problem I faced was how to discard the little bastard and become a new person.

I knew one thing for certain. If I stayed in my parents' house, I wouldn't make any headway at all. I needed rescuing. I needed a miracle. I remembered Auntie used to pray at all hours of the day and night. So I earnestly put my hands together to beg God for deliverance. And, as usually happens with me, I soon got what I asked for; though the miracle took a most unexpected form.

Father had got himself a new job that involved travelling around the country. Or so I was told. I suspect my parents were considering divorce. Whatever the truth, Father wasn't home much that summer. One morning a few days after I decided to be an artist I heard an awful racket in the kitchen. Curious to see what the noise was about I went out and poked my head around the door.

My little sister was writhing on the floor. Her mouth was foaming and her eyes had rolled back in her head. She kicked a chair over as she thrashed violently about. A glass got knocked off the table and it smashed spectacularly. I knew I'd get the blame for that. I turned around to hide in my room and there was Mother standing right behind me. She slapped me hard across the face.

'What have you done this time?' she growled.

Before I could protest she caught sight of my sister. Her face drained of colour like the time she'd seen the green tree-man sitting on the mango branch beside me. Mother was on the phone in moments. Then she was cradling my sister on the floor trying to calm the awful contortions. I stood and watched. It was a fascinating sight to behold.

The ambulance arrived. Mother and sister were swept up and taken away. I was left alone locked in the house for the rest of the day.

Some time after sunset Auntie turned up at the front door. I wouldn't let her in at first. I liked being alone and I didn't want my peace shattered with her silly chatter. After a long while she convinced me to unlock the door so she could talk to me.

She hugged me close. Naturally I screamed until she let me go.

'Your sister's very ill,' she told me with tears in her eyes.

'I know. I saw her. She was foaming at the mouth. I thought she was going to throw up.'

'She had a convulsion.'

'I know. I was there when it happened. I saw the whole thing.'

I was very calm but I've never liked being talked down to and Auntie talked down to everyone.

'You must be in shock,' she soothed. 'You poor thing.'

'Is she dead yet?'

My sister wasn't dead. They'd found she had a hole in her heart. She was going to have an operation to repair the damage. Auntie fried some potatoes for my dinner, but I didn't eat them. She made me a cup of tea and she sat at the table crying. That was the first time I ever drank a cup of tea and the first time she ever spoke with me at length.

I later found out that she'd been warned off approaching me. Father didn't like her. He'd had no time for her since she'd become a born-again Christian.

After Auntie calmed down a little she asked me about myself. I told her unashamedly that I had trouble shitting. I was testing her. I'd been told so much about her that was negative, I just wanted to gauge her reaction. When she asked me why I had problems with the toilet, I told her about the bad people.

She explained that what I'd encountered were spirits. 'Sometimes they're bad,' she said, 'and sometimes they're good. The bad ones come from Satan and the good ones come from God.'

She told me that Satan had no power over God, so I shouldn't be afraid of the bad spirits. The good spirits worked for God, so I certainly shouldn't be afraid of them. Her well-meaning, if naïve, explanation settled a lot of fear in me.

I told her about the blackfella and she replied that they used to turn up when she was my age. There was a dancing ring on her farm where they once conducted their ceremonies. Her husband built a chicken shed on top of it to stop them coming around.

Then I told her about the green tree-man. And I swear, all the blood drained from her face. 'That wasn't a man,' Auntie replied, dramatically. 'That was Satan. This may explain your terrible affliction.'

She grabbed me by the shoulders in an over-the-top theatrical gesture and I was so bewildered that for once I didn't scream.

'You must never talk to Satan. Do you understand? He is the Deceiver. The Dark One. He is the Devil; Lord of the Demons.' She was always going on like that. Poor deluded woman. If only she'd spoken about God a bit more now and then I might have been able to take her seriously.

I can't recall all the titles she had for Satan but I remember it was a fairly impressive list. I thought he must be a really bad bloke if he'd earned so many titles. With my hand on my heart I promised I wouldn't talk to the Dark One ever again.

She taught me a prayer called the 'Our Father'. But in typical fashion I misunderstood the words and for years afterwards I believed God's name was Harold – *Our Father who art in Heaven, Harold be thy name.*

That night I was taken to Nanna-Father's house to sleep. I hadn't visited her much before that. She preferred to be left alone and she had a reputation for being cranky. I didn't expect her to want me cluttering up her poky little home but she welcomed me warmly. I ended up staying there a few days and enjoying every minute of my visit. She was the first person I'd ever met who was anything like me.

She used to collect hundreds of paper bags which she folded neatly, ironed flat then stored in every spare drawer in the house. With a wink she showed me a big ammunition box full of old ten-shilling notes that she'd been saving. Australia had adopted a new decimal currency a few years earlier so they were really just worthless scraps of paper. Nanna-Father also talked to herself all the time.

Next morning I had a whole new life. Nanna-Father kept silkworms and she spun golden thread from their cocoons. She had old things – an ancient clock which she wound up every evening and a pedal sewing machine for making clothes. Her hair was silver-grey like the trunk of the gum tree that grew by the creek. At night she unbound her locks and let them fall. Her hair was so long it almost reached the ground. She asked me to brush it for her.

Nanna-Father showed me a picture of her family gathered around the wooden slab hut her father had built when he'd first arrived from Ireland. There were naked Aborigines standing to one side leaning on their spears. Nanna-Father was a young girl with long, golden hair. She pointed to a sapling in the picture.

'That's the big gum tree,' she said.

There was a huge chest of drawers in her main room that had a mirror above it. She called it her mantelpiece. All the treasures she'd collected in her life were arrayed along the top. I climbed up on a chair to get a better look at the ornaments.

The first thing I saw made me gasp with fright.

'It's the Deceiver!' I cried. 'You've got the Dark One on your mantelpiece.'

'What are you talking about, you stupid boy?'

I pointed to a beautifully crafted green glass snake that sat curled up in a purple glass bowl.

'I know who you've been talking to,' she snapped. 'That's not the Devil. It's just a glass snake.'

I told her what Auntie had said about my encounter with the green tree-man. Nanna-Father laughed and called her daughter a bloody fool. I told her about Father cutting up the snake and how I'd gone back to the mango tree to retrieve the skin.

'Do you know what the snake represents?' she asked me. 'We're all like snakes. Do you know what happens when you die?'

I shook my head.

'We shed ourselves. When we die we throw off all our worn out skin, the same way a snake does. Then we're renewed.'

She showed me her silkworms. She explained that every creature is a spirit trapped within a body. She told me caterpillars spend their lives gorging themselves on food. They're slow, dull creatures ruled by their stomachs. Eventually they spin a cocoon for themselves, made of the finest silk. Then they seem to die. But it isn't really death. Inside their silken shell they're transformed, and when the time is right they burst forth with wings and take to the air to dance with others of their kind.

'We're just like caterpillars,' she assured me. 'Each of us will have wings one day.'

Her explanation formed the basis for my later understanding of life. But it wasn't until later that night as I lay on her bedroom floor wrapped in blankets that I realised Nanna-Father had given me the answer I'd been looking for.

If a snake could shed its skin, then so could I. If a caterpillar could grow wings, then that's what I'd do. I'd grow wings and I'd fly away from Mother and I'd never come back.

Nanna-Father and I never got to spend much time together again. She preferred to be alone and the family weren't much bothered with her. She passed away while I was working in Spain years later. I heard that Auntie smashed the beautiful glass snake and trampled it into the dirt. It had been a source of bitter dispute between them for many years.

After my few days with Nanna-Father I spent a couple of nights with Auntie and Uncle. My short stay with Nanna-Father gave me a new perspective on Auntie. She was always moaning on about the wages of sin and the darkness that dwells in the hearts of men.

She reckoned I'd been afflicted as a punishment for speaking to a snake. When I refused to be hugged, she told me I was silly. When I would not to go to church, she assured me I was destined to burn in Hell. When I screamed, she proclaimed that I was possessed by a demon. Several times in my teenage years she offered to have me exorcised of the evil creature within but I always declined.

Auntie eventually informed me that my sister needed peace and quiet if she was to make a full recovery. It was decided that I'd be sent to stay with relatives on the other side of town.

I was nervous about leaving my familiar surroundings, but I was also very excited. When my relatives picked me up, it was noticed I was still sporting bruises on my face that Mother had inflicted.

The house I was to stay in belonged to Mother's eldest sister, who I addressed as Auntie-Sister.

Auntie-Sister put cold cloths on my bruises and gave me lemonade. Her house was a palace. The whole time I was there no one threatened to beat me. No one called me an idiot. No one so much as swore at me or raised their voice.

Auntie-Sister was a good cook, a very good cook. She let me help her in the kitchen and taught me a few important secrets about cooking. I *tasted* food for the first time, instead of just eating it. I began to enjoy mealtimes.

After staying with Auntie-Sister I could never stomach Mother's bland burnt offerings again. There were herbs and fresh vegetables in Auntie-Sister's pantry. Sweet breads, spicy sauces and rice were on the menu, as often as a traditional Australian roast dinner. I was in Heaven. I decided that cooking would be one of the skills I'd have to master.

While I lived with Auntie-Sister I started to get the hang of going to the toilet. I was still very uncomfortable about it but I managed to put aside my fears and get on with it.

Part of the reason was that I had a new understanding of the spirits. Once I had an explanation for the fear I was feeling, it was much easier to ignore the bad people. Spirits were gradually relegated to my dreams after that. The other thing was that Auntie-Sister had a toilet inside the house. It was a flush toilet in a big closet that offered me the privacy I needed and craved.

I met cousins I'd never encountered before and I was made to feel like an important member of the family. People asked my opinion. I still didn't sleep at night and I couldn't stand to be touched, but I had a really good rest.

At home there was a constant threat from Mother's temper. At Auntie-Sister's I was given drawing paper, pencils, artist's pastels and paints. I sat in the window box fascinated by the sunlight on the stained glass window. I could sleep all day if I wanted to and stay up all night.

I went for long walks with her husband. I was allowed to go off wandering in the bush by myself. I smiled so much my face ached. I even went swimming in a big creek and loved every minute of it.

The best thing of all was that I was introduced to cats. Auntie-Sister's cat had a litter of kittens the week before I turned up. I was given a bunk bed in a little room out the back that used to be a kitchen. The cat decided to keep her kittens under the covers with me. In fact she'd go off for long periods and leave me to watch after them.

I learned cat language very quickly. I liked cats from the very start. I noticed they were a lot like me. Cats hate being looked in the eye. Eye contact is a threat to them. They'll glance at you occasionally and they don't mind you doing the same but don't stare too much or they'll walk away from you.

Cats don't like being picked up and stroked unless it's on their terms. They prefer to initiate any physical contact. And they can be very cranky if things don't go their way; often turning suddenly violent if you overstep the boundaries with them. They're aloof and forthright. They revel in their privacy, their independence and their freedom. They love to play, and they're often awake at night. My introduction to cats opened up a whole world of understanding for me.

That was the best summer I'd ever had. I didn't want to go home. When Father came to pick me up I immediately commenced the process of shut-down. All the way home he lectured me about how it was my fault my little sister had almost died. He told me I was a little bastard and that if my behaviour didn't improve I'd be put in a boys' home for the rest of my life.

'I'm going to be good,' I assured him. 'I'm an artist.'

'You're a bloody retard.'

By the time we arrived at the house I was completely numb again.

My sister's health improved quickly. She didn't look sickly to me any more. I entered third grade but school wasn't important. It was just something distasteful I had to endure if I didn't want to end up in the lunatic asylum. I discovered the library and began thumbing through picture books about history and art, but I wasn't interested in reading so I didn't bother with the words.

I displayed my artworks proudly to Mother to begin with. She took great delight in setting fire to my most treasured pieces. So I had to practise drawing and calligraphy in secret. Auntie-Sister had given me a model aeroplane for Christmas and I treasured it. I must have put it together and taken it apart a dozen times.

I spent more and more of my life in my room. I got used to shutting the door. I had to cut myself off in order to allow my new identity to develop. Becoming an artist was like trying on different masks. I'd adopt new traits and habits for a while to try them out, discarding those I didn't like and keeping the ones that worked.

I was guided by what other people thought was right and wrong. I didn't feel I was entitled to make up my own mind about it. At nine I still felt compelled to tear off my clothes and run around naked to ease the itching burn of cloth. But by ten years of age I'd managed to bring that under control to a greater extent. I was determined to be a good boy.

· What had happened to me was that I'd become an obedient dog. All I wanted to do was please everyone. I kept my head down and tried not to draw too much attention to myself. However, Mother wasn't prepared to let this sleeping dog lie. She was always coming up with some new drama to blame me for. There was always an excuse to dish out a beating.

I was led to believe I was becoming more and more difficult. It's true I could fly off the handle if my routine was disturbed or if my surroundings were tampered with; but that was happening less and less. Of course, Mother took a perverse delight in hiding my favourite books or springing a dental appointment on me at short notice.

I hated the dentist. He had bad breath. I told him so.

I said to him, 'Never trust a dentist with bad breath.'

Perhaps in revenge he filled all my teeth even though they didn't need the work. I saw him as a simple-minded, greedy liar. Gradually as I got older I began to suspect that the problems I encountered with others weren't always exclusively my fault.

The next three years passed by quickly and I have little recollection of anything significant that may have happened. I was shut down most of the time, off in my own little Far Country, isolated from others while I honed my skills as an artist.

Outside of my room I lived in a kind of waking sleep. I was just going through the motions. I'd even given up on the idea of escape. Mother had learned from Pop all about breaking horses and children. She'd broken my spirit. I'd given up trying to make any show of defiance. I just wanted to please her.

My imagination was the only part of me she couldn't touch. It was my secret. I suppose that's why I shut down. It was the only way to keep my secret safe.

Brisbane was a growing city, but it was a bleak, boring, soul-less place. There wasn't enough stimulation for someone like me. I had a burning desire to learn about art, music, theatre and to test my own creativity. I was hungry for challenges that the school system simply couldn't offer. I despaired in the midst of that cultural desert.

In the few moments when I was awake enough to realise my predicament I sometimes wished I was dead. I was desperate to shed my skin and move on, but with every advance I made in changing myself I faced another setback. I relapsed into the old pattern of tearing my clothes off.

I went to the doctor about an earache when I was 12 years old. It was the same doctor who'd advised Mother to beat me until I begged forgiveness and to stick a rolling pin up my backside to frighten me. On this occasion he offered the opinion that I'd turned out very effeminate and far too pretty for a boy. He speculated that I might be homosexual. He quoted some crank American psychologist who claimed that autistic boys are more likely to turn out homosexual. He reckoned it was why I insisted on tearing my clothes off. I was an exhibitionist, a sexual pervert.

These days it's difficult to imagine how devastating all this talk might have been back in the early seventies in a backward town in ultra-conservative Australia. Besides the obvious social stigma attached to homosexuality, it was also illegal in Queensland. Homosexual men were typically imprisoned for 15 years with hard labour. To the best of my knowledge I'd never encountered a homosexual. I didn't even know what it meant, except that it was a very bad thing to be called.

Mother immediately stepped up the physical punishment again, though I never encountered the rolling pin again. Father took to regularly beating me as well. He saw it as his duty and considered it to be for my own good. Mother mentioned years later that she sincerely believed thrashing me would curb my unnatural sexual tendencies. She'd already been led to believe that physical punishment could cure me of autism, so it made perfect sense to her.

It was bad enough, she often said, to have a retarded son. She wasn't going to have me turn out to be a poofter as well. Poofter is seventies Australian slang for a homosexual. No one would dare use that word today; it's so politically incorrect.

Autism was explained to me by that same doctor as a kind of sexual deviation combined with psychotic and anti-social tendencies. He told me that autistics are unable to conform to what society defines as normal. He reckoned that I'd turn out to be a compulsive liar and probably end up in prison like most autistic men. I began to be ashamed for crimes I hadn't committed, didn't understand and hadn't even had an opportunity to contemplate.

Father didn't say much to me for nearly two years, not even when he was laying into me with the strap. Mother later explained to me that it had all been very hard on him. Up to then he'd been in denial about my problems. He'd still held out the hope that I'd get better and be able to carry on his family tradition in the Masonic Lodge.

'But the Masons don't accept retards or homos,' Mother informed me. 'You broke his heart.'

Auntie-Sister was so shocked to hear about my alleged homosexuality that she didn't speak to me again until a few brief words passed between us at Mother's funeral. Pop barred me from his house. I rarely saw Nanna again until after Pop died. The few people I felt close to were completely cut off from me.

I was forbidden to have friends, especially male friends. This wasn't too difficult to bear. I've never got on well with males and at the time I had no one of my own age I felt close to. Mother was the only person I ended up having much contact with.

At the time I was so ashamed of myself I just accepted that I'd done the wrong thing and that this situation was all my fault. No one ever bothered to ask me if I was homosexual. No one thought my opinion was worth inquiring after. Without any experience of the world I accepted the authority of a dubious quack who'd expressed an equally dubious opinion.

Not only was I considered to be a homosexual, I was also branded a sexual deviant. Yet there was no evidence for any of this. I'm not sexually attracted to men and I never have been. As a boy of 12 I couldn't articulate that, but I pointed it out to Mother during our last conversation. She breathed a sigh of relief and admitted she'd always wondered whether or not she'd gone far enough with the beatings. She passed away content that she'd saved me from a life of sexual perversity.

This issue couldn't have arisen at a worse time. I'd just started to get confident about reinventing myself. I was reaching puberty and facing all the confusion that brings. This bogus accusation, presented as an authoritative medical diagnosis, had an awful effect on me. I withdrew ever further into myself for shame.

Within a few months I started eighth grade, the first year of high school. Mother decided I needed to be toughened up so I was sent to a very rough school of over 1500 students. The endless round of bullying that had tapered off in grade six and seven suddenly returned with renewed viciousness. My naïveté and my state of intermittent shut-down made me an easy target.

From the very first day I was taunted with 'dickhead' and 'retard'. I'd expected no less. But to my embarrassment and dismay I was also being called a poofter. In the afternoon I'd walk home barely holding back the tears.

I was so ashamed of myself I'd lock myself in my bedroom, sit at the window and wish the world would end. I soon realised that other parents were not like mine. At high school I met young people who were very similar to me in many respects but their lives couldn't have been more different from mine. They were comfortable with who they were. Their parents supported them. They weren't beaten up for being themselves; no matter how eccentric they seemed to be. Some of them went out of their way to appear different from the majority.

I was seething with inexpressible anger at the injustice of my position. I started to wonder how much I'd been lied to. I began to doubt the doctors and psychologists who'd played such a prominent role in shaping my life.

A few months into the year I received confirmation that the world wasn't all it seemed to be. The doctor who'd diagnosed me as a homosexual was arrested and charged with sexually assaulting one of his patients – a teenage boy. He was the same learned gentleman who'd convinced Mother to shove a rolling pin up my arse to cure me of my rages. His motives for labelling me homosexual were never questioned, nor was his diagnosis.

★ ★ ★

As that year progressed Father sold the block of land next door. The mango tree was cut down. I caressed the precious snakeskin as I watched strange men cut the tree into tiny logs and throw the whole lot on a roaring bonfire. I sobbed for the green tree-man and withdrew into renewed guilt for his death.

After that I retreated further and further into my dreams and fantasies where I could be whoever I wanted to be without being punished or hounded for my ways. I practised calligraphy day and night. I became very interested in medieval history, especially the Holy Grail. At some point I solemnly dedicated my life to the search for it. I had no idea what it was. A vague image of a golden cup persisted in my head.

I was so naïve. I had the notion that if I drank from the Sacred Chalice I'd be granted healing and eternal life. I don't know where I got that wild idea but for many years I earnestly and wholeheartedly believed it. I suppose it gave me something to hope for. My interest in the Holy Grail led me to attempt reading the Bible, but I found the whole thing too implausible, poorly written and contradictory. I gave up trying to understand it before I got to the end of Genesis.

I discovered *The Goon Show*, a classic BBC radio comedy. I could mimic the many voices perfectly. I especially loved the characters Peter Sellers played. I would call up whole episodes from my memory and recite every line, smoothly moving from one character to the next. However, the only thing I hated about *The Goon Show* was the 1950s jazz they played during the intermission.

I coveted old records and convincingly mimicked singers such as Bing Crosby and Dean Martin. Though I wasn't permitted to listen to evil pop music on the radio, I used to switch on my crystal set late at night with the headphones squeezed to my ears in the hope of catching songs by the Beatles, the Rolling Stones and the Kinks. John Lennon's singing voice entered my repertoire.

When not engaged in pursuits that interested me, I was a passive zombie who rarely spoke unless taunted. I managed to keep my personal passions alive by adopting various masks that I could take off and hide away where no one could find them. To begin with I only wore the masks in private, but gradually my other personas drifted into my real life.

I came to call these masks 'characters'. They were like the voices on *The Goon Show*. That's exactly how I saw my personas, as characters in a play. All the world's a stage, as Will Shakespeare put it. One of my early characters wore glasses, though I certainly didn't need to wear spectacles so he soon discarded them and transformed himself. I came to know him as Feeble.

Another character began collecting waistcoats and 1930s clothes. He spoke very formally and was reminiscent of Pop. He was a rebel who remained a constant in my life through my university years. He's since branched out into pocket-watches and Victorian frock coats. Lately the Rebel has been coming out to play more and more. He didn't have a name back then. He wasn't completely formed.

There was another strange character as well. Right from the start I called him the Mahjee. I don't know where I got that name from; it just came to me one day. The Mahjee was a wise man, an old soul. The Mahjee was forgiving and calm; he was patient and quietly confident. Everyone respected him and he had many friends. The Mahjee was the first character to really solidify and stick. He possessed all the qualities I was told I could never have.

At school I couldn't make head or tail of the timetable so I was always late to class. I used to get in terrible trouble for that. Once or twice I got the cuts. I hated the cuts. Not because of the pain. It was the embarrassment – shame was affecting me very deeply. Teachers told me I'd never amount to anything and I believed it.

I'd had the notion nailed to my head that I was defective, disabled and less-than-human. So I reached the conclusion I had nothing to lose by taking a stand. The Mahjee started speaking out about the stupidity and hypocrisy of the cuts. To my surprise a few other students stood up and agreed. Not just students came forward – one or two teachers quietly voiced their support. I was becoming known as a bit of a rebel.

One day during English class the Rebel gave an impassioned speech against Australia's involvement in the Vietnam War. I was sent to the office for that. Later he spoke against the logging of native forests, long before environmental issues were fashionable. He decried the bigotry and racism of the state government who were talking about sterilising all male Aborigines. I was warned to keep quiet or I'd be sent to Goodna.

Mention of that place was enough to snuff out the last sparks of resistance in me. I removed the rebel mask and stepped out of that character into a kind of void where I had no personality. However, the Rebel stayed with me in the background. I'd made my first steps into the world so there was to be no going back. I'd tasted an alternative to shut-down and, though there were obviously risks involved, I found my characters exhilarating.

I was so terrified about being imprisoned I believe I had a kind of nervous breakdown around that time. I can't be sure as there's a long period where everything went blank. I don't remember much of what happened. I guess the rest of the year I went dumbly about my life. I talked to no one except myself for a long while.

In the middle of the night around Christmas time that year I got up out of bed. It was one of those draining summer nights that sap the strength out of you. I went to the window to catch the breeze and smell the coming rain.

The sky was lit by the brilliant purples of a tremendous tropical storm. Thunder rolled in, rocking the timbers of the house so much the roof-tiles rattled and the floor shook. I did something I'd never done before. I swung open my window and stuck my head out into the rain. Huge drops, as heavy as hail, pelted down and stung my face. Then a great spear of violet light descended from the heavens with a mighty crack that knocked me backwards into the mosquito net as it struck the very top branches of the gum tree.

For a few brief moments I sat on the floor of my bedroom unable to move. Then I caught sight of an awesome orange glow outside. When I got up I saw that the whole top of the eucalypt was on fire. I ran outside into the paddock, oblivious of the danger from lightning. The rain had turned to icy hail and it fell hard on me, driving me back to the shelter of the house.

I stood under the awning screaming and hopping impatiently about until the squall subsided. Then I ran down to the gum tree and threw my arms about it to comfort it in its dying moments. Burning leaves, bark and embers fell down upon me. I smelled burning hair and the soles of my feet were in pain; but I ignored all that.

In a split second the tree that had been a sapling when Nanna-Father was a girl, the tree I'd thought would always be there when I looked out the window, was taken away from me. I swear to you I felt the life draining out of it as its spirit shed skin and took to the wing. The wind snatched up glowing ashes into the air that started spot fires in the bush. I was sobbing.

The next thing I knew Father grabbed me by the throat. Then he was violently dragging me back toward the house. I struggled against him and he punched me hard in the guts, winding me. I remember staggering up the stairs to the door. Mother threw a blanket over me. Until that moment I hadn't noticed I was completely naked. After that the rain fell in bucket-loads, as it only can in the tropics. And when all the gum leaves had burned away the fire finally went out.

I woke up next morning feeling refreshed and renewed. The sun was shining brightly and there wasn't a cloud in the sky. I thought I must have been dreaming about the fire and the storm. Then I looked out the window at the blackened stump of the old gum tree. To this day I can't be sure how much of that night was a dream and how much actually happened. It was one of the strangest experiences of my life.

The death of my gum tree signalled many changes. The coming year looked like being as mundane and pointless as the one that had just passed. I prayed for deliverance and once again a wondrous miracle unfolded. As is usual with me this miracle was completely unexpected and unlooked for. I thought I caught a glimpse of the Holy Grail.

Four

Recently I've spoken to psychologists who specialise in helping adults who exhibit autism spectrum attributes. I've heard from folks my own age who've been diagnosed as autistic and I've been surprised at how similarly we view the world. I've also canvassed the views of many other people who don't show signs of autism. As a result of all this research I've begun to understand that my experience of life is quite different from the majority of people.

For a start I perceive my surroundings as an intense flood of sensual information received by highly attuned sensory organs. The Flood only subsides when I sleep deeply or shut down. From my point of view the Flood is a normal state so it's hard for me to be objective about it. So here's a few examples of how my senses work.

Hearing. I can identify species and occasionally gender from a distant bird call. At five years of age I could barely speak. At the same time I was beginning to mimic the cries of native Australian wildlife very precisely. As I got older this ability for mimicry extended to foreign accents. I learn languages very quickly – sometimes within weeks if I'm inspired and have the opportunity to practise. I can hear a piece of music once and usually improvise around the main theme on any of the instruments I'm proficient at.

Vision. Compared to most people I know I'm extraordinarily long-sighted. I have an eye for detail. Colours evoke intense emotional reactions in me that may lead to laughter, tears, headaches, nausea or elation amongst other responses. Colour and flavour are intricately woven together for me; so much so that I can't imagine what it would be like to experience one without the other.

Sense of smell. I can pick the scents of most animals, especially the musky odours of Australian marsupials. I can also identify particular humans I know by their individual scents. Indeed, I will recognise friends by their scents before I see their faces. I can literally smell fear on a person or animal, and this can set me off into a terrible panic.

The perfumes of native wildflowers and the rainforest give me indescribable joy, but my greatest nose-love would have to be essential oils. I have a huge collection of oils in neatly-labelled, little brown bottles. I delight in all things olfactory, but oils conjure pleasurable sensory overloads that stimulate my whole physical being. My favourite at the moment is the ancient aroma of sacred spikenard. It reminds me of Morocco. I never tracked one down that smells of camel-shit. I have the old jalabah for that. I drag it out every once in a while and with one whiff I can almost feel a knife at my throat.

Taste. This sense is very demanding. I love spices and full-flavoured food. I can't stand bland fare. Mother was a hopelessly incompetent cook who never varied her recipes. She used to boil meat, potatoes, carrots, spinach and peas together in a pressure cooker until they were reduced to a grey tasteless mess of unpalatable mush which she had the misplaced confidence to call soup.

Day after day, week after week, she served the same meals again and again. The boredom was unbearable. Supper was a time of despair for me and I rarely finished a meal Mother put down in front of me. I'm certain her unique flair for murdering flavour is the main reason I wasn't all that interested in eating when I was young. On the other hand, she inspired me to obsessively study the art of cooking. Before I was 20 I'd learned how to make each meal a satisfying and pleasurable experience.

Touch. This is the sense I was most punished for indulging as a child and as a result it's the one I'm most inhibited and confused about these days. Clothes were an unbearable experience for me and still can be. Even today I may be caught unawares by the urge to disrobe at an inappropriate time. However, I don't usually act on it for fear of the consequences.

I experience colours, sounds, scents and taste woven together with touch. I'm working on rolling back my inhibitions about this most intense and private of all my senses but I fear the damage was done very early.

These are the senses for which I have names. There are other senses operating in me as well. I can often perceive when a person is lying, angry, sad, frustrated, annoyed, frightened or anxious. I'm told the word for this is empathy.

My definition of empathy is the full fury of all my senses firing off at once. It's the storm of empathy that overwhelms me. However, empathy and the other senses are as nothing compared to emotional overload.

Emotional events are the most devastating and rewarding occurrences I have to deal with each day. For example, when I allow love to take hold of me I will cry; I will be almost incapacitated, shaking with joy. When I'm frightened I'll shake in much the same way. In fact if I were to allow my emotions to ravage me with their full impact, I would be a shaking mess most of the time.

When I was a little child I used to let my emotions rule over me completely. If I felt angry, I'd let the full force of it wash over and out of me. This may go some way to explaining my rages. My parents and the psychologists considered these rages inappropriate, but they were my way of dealing with frustration. As soon as the rage had burned out, it was forgotten and so was the cause.

The beatings temporarily cured me of rages and taught me to hold in my emotions, like a good little boy. Most people I know withhold their emotions very well and without too much effort. I managed to retain my punishment-reinforced conditioning until I was in my mid-20s but I decided it didn't work well enough for me.

I found it was far healthier to release my emotions in the Flood rather than bottle them up until I became so frustrated I exploded. Nowadays I put much of my emotion into the composition of quite complex and moving pieces of music. From bitter experience I've learned that anger is one emotion in particular that is better expressed than kept under lock and key.

I find that the release of anger when it arises allows me to move on from the problem that caused it in the first place. If I let it out, I'm incapable of holding on to a grudge. So, if I'm angry with someone I tend not to hold back. I let it rip. Fortunately the people closest to me understand and accept that this is my way.

When I'm swamped by a rush of information, be it sensory or emotional, I simply shut down my sensory inputs and emotional outputs. Most of the time there's nothing I can do about it; it's an involuntary reaction.

Shut-down is a spectrum of responses. At the mild end I may partially close myself off to another person if I'm feeling uncomfortable or suspicious about their motives. The slightest hint of threat, rebuke or ridicule is enough to initiate this response. In other words, it can happen in almost any social situation where I don't feel I'm on solid ground with the people around me.

To those who don't know me well it may appear as if I don't respond appropriately in social situations. I've spent a lifetime as a virtual recluse because I don't like upsetting people or being attacked for my weirdness. This isolation has compounded the problem. Anyone who bothers to look past this minor glitch of mine soon realises it's not such a big deal.

At the other end of the spectrum I may shut down completely and lapse into a catatonic state. This last happened to me a few years ago when my cat, Angus, passed away. He'd been the only steady friend in my life in 16 years. He was my only family. The grief was so unbearable I simply sat frozen on the sofa for three days until the pain began to ease. It took me months to recover from his death.

A few years back a psychologist I was seeing told me that autistics don't understand even the simplest social signals and emotions. For me this certainly isn't true and I suspect I'm not Robinson Crusoe in that regard.

The severe punishment regimes I was subjected to were intended to modify my behaviour and make me fit to engage with mainstream society. This was a common practice in the sixties and seventies. Punitive measures were thought to be the only sure way to cure autism, as if autism is a disease. The barbaric practice of behaviour modification was endorsed by psychologists and health professionals who would nowadays blush at their former enthusiasm for it.

In the seventies I saw a documentary on television about how Goodna Mental Hospital was pioneering the use of electric shock therapy in curing everything from smoking to homosexuality. I believe this regime is becoming fashionable again in the United States. The thought of it makes me shiver.

In my early teens I came to view conformists as frightened individuals with limited imaginations and no respect for the individuality of others. I observed them trying to categorise, standardise and subdue their surroundings and everyone they met. By then I'd had a lot of experience with fear so perhaps I wasn't as terrified of the world as some people seemed to be.

Today I consider attempts by one section of society to force conformity on another as pathetic, desperate exercises in manipulation. Some people just can't cope with life unless they feel they're in control. Such narrow, insecure folks will do anything to wrest control from others. That includes marginalising and confining others in ideological prisons, if not prisons made of bricks and mortar.

I concede that, to a certain extent, punishment worked very well on me. I'm extremely well-trained. I obey orders and take criticism to heart. I do as I'm told and I go out of my way to make those around me happy and comfortable. My whole life has been focused on making myself a better person and being good.

However, the price I've paid for conformity has been enormous. All the time I wasted looking for a cure for myself certainly could have been better spent. I suffer constant stress from the need to do the right thing because the definitions of 'good' and 'right' are different for everyone I know. And the definitions are constantly shifting. For the better part of my life I was no more than a chameleon with no will, ambition or desires of my own. To a certain extent I still am.

Hindsight is a wonderful thing, but at the beginning of my 13th year I didn't understand I was a chameleon. I was a zombie with no sense of self or hope for the future. Only rare faint glimmers of inspiration kept me going.

Things changed when Father convinced me to join the Air Training Corps, the cadet reserves of the Air Force. They met every weekend at a local parade-ground. He thought it would toughen me up. He reckoned it'd knock the poofter out of me.

I learned how to march. I learned how to survive in the bush, find water, light a fire and navigate by the stars. I learned what poofter meant. It was described to me in great detail by my peers, some of whom were defensively disguising their sexuality beneath layers of bravado.

I became fascinated with rifles when I discovered I had a natural talent as a marksman. I appreciated the order a military life offered. But all the intricate rules of behaviour were beyond me. My fellow cadets seemed frustratingly simple-minded.

I had the opportunity to fly in a combat helicopter with a battle-hardened crew who'd just returned from Vietnam. I was seated in the starboard gunner's position with the doors wide open. As soon as we took off the pilot started flipping the aircraft around like it was a trick yo-yo. Only a flimsy seat-belt prevented me from being thrown out.

One moment I'd see nothing but blue sky; the next there'd be a herd of cows that looked so close I could almost reach out and touch them. It was the scariest thing I'd done up to that point. When the machine landed I threw myself down on the field on my hands and knees and spewed up my breakfast until there was nothing left in my stomach but bile.

I couldn't specifically pinpoint what frightened me about the ride. The pilot was one of the best. He'd been doing that sort of thing for years in a war zone with Vietcong shells bursting all around him. I couldn't have been in safer hands really when you think about it.

I came to the conclusion that death didn't bother me too much. I mean it couldn't have been that much worse than my life, could it? My flight in an attack helicopter got me very interested in the nature of terror. I decided, as an experiment, that I'd set about challenging my fears.

For all the positive things I learned in the Air Training Corps I also suffered the worst bullying of my life. I was brutalised for being a pretty-boy poofter and I was ridiculed by the flight-sergeant for being slow on the uptake. My fellow cadets looked on me with suspicion because I didn't enthusiastically support the war. They were all hoping it would go on until they were old enough to fight. I saw the whole conflict as futile.

At school I was enrolled on courses that had been chosen for me by Mother. I hated every subject I was forced to take. I started missing classes I didn't like, which was almost every one, except English. In that class I was encouraged to speak freely.

As it happened my English teacher fell ill halfway through the year and a student teacher took over for a few weeks. She was in her early twenties, blonde, slim, intelligent and very confident. She took an immediate shine to me. She told me she liked my stance against the war and the cane. We shared an interest in a comedy team who called themselves Monty Python. I called my teacher-friend, Miss.

We spent a few afternoons talking after school finished and I grew to feel comfortable in her company. Before she went back to college she told me she knew I was autistic and that I was having difficulties. It was on my record. A tentative trust had built between us. I appreciated that she was so open with me. And naturally I felt attracted to her, as any heterosexual 13-year-old boy would have been.

One night in a dream Miss appeared before me dressed in a long white robe. There was a halo around her head and she held a silver cup before her in both hands. She offered it to me and I drank the water from it. She said, 'You're healed.' Then as I held the cup she slipped the robes from her shoulder and stood naked before me. At my shoulder I felt a piercing, agonising pain. It was so severe I had to look down. There was a claw digging into my flesh. Miss held a mirror up to me and I saw a small dragon clinging to my back. It flicked its tongue and reminded me of the green tree-man. I was suddenly ashamed to be standing before my naked teacher and I turned away. The dream ended and I sat up wide awake with an unfamiliar tingling in my groin. That was my first glimpse of the Holy Grail, my first encounter with a naked woman and my first meeting with the shame-dragon.

I was so deeply brainwashed into believing everything everyone told me about myself that it took a few more months for me to wake up to the idea that I obviously wasn't homosexual. When I came to that realisation I had some extremely bitter and angry moments.

It was a shock to realise I'd been punished, victimised and attacked for being something I was not. It seemed as if my legitimate defects were not enough for some people; they had to invent more to taunt me with. By the end of that year I was calling into question everything I'd been told about myself.

At that stage I really didn't understand that I'd been brutalised or traumatised. Conventional wisdom dictated that shell-shock was something soldiers suffered from, not teenage boys. I thought my strangeness was the cause of all my problems. It was my fault and that was all there was to it.

The next year would have been more of the same, but Australia had a change of government and that had a profound effect on me. Australian troops were immediately withdrawn from Vietnam and all things military became decidedly unfashionable. The Air Training Corps was disbanded.

In uniform at cadets I'd been allowed to forget I was autistic, retarded and strange. No one ever discussed it with me. I'd begun to practise covering up my weird ways as if I could lock autism in the cellar of my soul and forget about it. Denial can be a very sweet treat. I was desperate to continue experiencing the same kind of freedom I'd known in the Air Training Corps. I also wanted to be able to continue target shooting and I'd begun to understand the importance of self-discipline. The military offered me an opportunity to explore a disciplined approach to life. Within weeks I'd signed up with one of a handful of naval cadet detachments that were permitted to continue operating.

Over the summer holidays I took up listening to short-wave radio programmes from around the world. I became obsessed with anything in French. I loved to hear the language spoken even though I couldn't understand a word of it. I got books out from the library and a French–English dictionary. In a couple of months I didn't need the books to help me any more. I could understand everything that was being said in French and I could spot regional dialects and accents.

The re-emergence of the Mahjee helped me immensely. If I wanted to achieve a goal, I'd simply hand over the controls of my life to him and he'd make the arrangements. All my life I'd been told I was stupid, useless, retarded, slow, mentally handicapped, so I didn't believe I could do anything by myself. The Mahjee, on the other hand was an extremely capable character who was able to strategise, plan and acquire new skills through a combination of willpower, intelligence and rigid self-discipline. When I was with the Mahjee I could read fluently and I could confidently research and absorb any subject.

Every night I tuned in the short-wave radio to hear comedies and documentaries in French and English. I heard newsreaders speaking

English with European and Asian accents. As I had done when I was younger, I began to mimic the newsreaders.

Suddenly I was coming out with all sorts of accents, so convincing that strangers often tried speaking to me in German, Japanese and Spanish. One day someone asked me in French what part of France I came from. To my own surprise I replied in perfect French that I was Australian. I'd picked up that much from the radio. Later that year a French ship came into port. I met some French sailors and ended up showing them around town. They told me before they left that they'd originally thought I was from Paris. My accent was so clear.

For me, 1975 was a great year. I began painting landscapes and surrealist portraits. I earned a marksman's badge for target shooting. I was chosen to take part in a ceremonial guard for the navy. I loved ceremonial and enthusiastically volunteered for guard drill whenever the chance came up. At this time I met so many new people from different walks of life. I was busy and my days were full. I was full of confidence. The Mahjee had stepped in to guide me and I'm so grateful that he did. I lost contact with the old retarded me for a long while. It was like being on an extended holiday.

My friend the teacher, who I called Miss, returned to school after she'd qualified to teach. I insisted in enrolling in one of her classes even though I wasn't at all interested in the subject. Over the next two years we got to know each other very well, often sharing jokes at the expense of my fellow students. She was a bit of a hippy and she introduced me to the idea of meditation.

I researched meditation techniques and this led me to read about Buddhism, which naturally appealed to the Mahjee. He loved the whole concept of reincarnation. It made much more sense than the narrow, fear-based, racist and intolerant attitudes of most Christians I knew.

Though I was frightened to death of going out to sea on a training ship the Mahjee was excited and keen for adventure. So he pushed the frightened me aside and took over completely. I trained as a gunnery rating in the naval cadets and I had a great time. No one knew the autistic me. I was getting better and better at covering me up.

I had a fresh start in life and I never discussed autism with any of my new acquaintances. Freed from the constraining definition of myself as faulty I began to bloom. The Mahjee was so good for me.

Mother told me before she died that I'd changed so dramatically around that time she hardly recognised me. She actually became afraid of me even though the rages I used to suffer from had subsided completely.

The psychologist decided that I'd suffered a mental collapse coupled with a severe identity crisis. My condition was deemed untreatable. He warned me not to become attached to anyone or to hold any expectations for my life. I needed to be institutionalised for my own safety. My name was put on another waiting list with a higher priority. I was informed that I would end up in a mental hospital in care and there was no way I could avoid it.

My parents didn't speak up on my behalf. They made it clear they were glad to be getting rid of me. In Mother's view I was a useless financial burden who would never be able to contribute to the household or take care of her in old age. They both washed their hands of me. So I made up my mind to enjoy myself while I still had my freedom.

An interesting thing happened with regard to my parents after that. I somehow developed a way of switching Mother and Father off to my senses and awareness. They simply ceased to exist for me while the Mahjee was in control. So 90 per cent of the frustration, annoyance and anger I'd been suffering up to that point was instantly dispelled. Perhaps that had something to do with the calming of my rage attacks.

Switching off others is a gift I have to this day. It comes in very handy when people overwhelm me with their cloying control agendas, their prejudice or their ridiculously low expectations. My entire life up to that point had been a series of manipulations instigated by Mother and Father. That's all behaviour modification and punitive treatment boil down to in my opinion: manipulation.

I've questioned a few psychologists about my ability to switch off. I've come to the conclusion that several factors were at work when I developed this aspect of my gifts.

The main trigger was trauma, but I'd also begun to understand that Mother and Father did not practise what they preached. They were hypocrites who didn't seem to care about anyone but themselves. And they weren't the only ones. I witnessed double-standards everywhere.

If it was good enough for others it was good enough for me. I embraced a character who was skilled at disguising the outward manifestations of autism. Before the Mahjee I'd stuttered whenever nervous. I'd been unable to initiate conversations or eye contact. I'd been deeply afraid of strangers and suspicious of everyone else. I consumed information on subjects that took my fancy and regurgitated it all at every opportunity. Yet I couldn't maintain interest in a conversation about mundane subjects I wasn't interested in.

The advent of the Mahjee raised my confidence levels to unprecedented heights. I was no longer self-conscious about the way I talked. I allowed my eccentric dress-sense free rein without worrying what others thought of me. I was wearing dress waistcoats and 19th-century frock coats when flares were still in fashion. The Rebel began to emerge again, though he tended to be quietly rebellious. He rarely spoke openly on political or social issues.

In order for the Mahjee to survive I had to completely expunge some people and their limited views from my awareness. Mother and Father were the first to go. I went on with my life separated more and more each day from the people who should have been supporting me and accepting me. I cooked my own meals, washed and immaculately ironed my own clothes, including my naval uniform.

By the time I turned 16 I had two distinct identities. There was the frightened, tainted autistic who was too traumatised to come out in the real world and as a result was relegated to dreams and nightmares. The Mahjee – my other identity – called him Feeble. That's the name I still have for my withered self. In fact, Feeble and the Mahjee are two aspects of the same character, but back then they still seemed independent. I've only recently recognised their close relationship to one another.

The Mahjee could do anything from rigging the sails on an eight-man skiff to learning languages and delivering well-rehearsed, impassioned, political speeches. No prizes for guessing who I preferred to hang out with.

When I enrolled in tenth grade at age 16 a third aspect of me suddenly and spectacularly emerged. This character used to be known as the Rebel, but he now called himself Charles P. Puddlejumper. He was a classic clown, a comedic yet embittered soul with an anarchic wit and a dangerous disregard for rules. I suspect he may have owed his origins to Peter Sellers and Monty Python.

Charles P. unexpectedly popped out for the first time during a spoken English assessment presided over by my teacher-friend, Miss. When it was my turn to speak he got up to present a lucid argument detailing how the twisted myth of monogamy, the dull prison of conformity and the fetish cult of materialism together had the potential to pervert the blessed gift of life.

I used the slogan 'monogamy, monopoly, monotony'. I'd picked that up from a radio discussion about the counter-culture. I warned my fellow students about the dangers of selling themselves into debt-slavery in return for a carbon-copy, crappy brick house in a bleak, uninspiring shit-hole like Brisbane.

Apart from the slogan I have no idea where that little rave originated. At the time I knew little of politics except what I'd heard on the television or radio. I'm sure Charles P. really didn't have a clue what he was talking about but it certainly felt good to let all my pent-up frustration erupt. It was a new kind of rage.

The other students were left in a state of stunned silence after he'd finished speaking. Miss asked me to stay after class when everyone else had gone. I expected to be severely reprimanded, but to my surprise she told me she was very proud of me. She shook my hand in congratulations and promised me it was going to be an interesting year. I nearly fainted from the intensity of her touch. All the way home my heart was in my throat.

You may have already guessed that Mr Puddlejumper didn't live in the same world as everyone else. He scorned the suburban ambitions of his peers. He could see no value in following the same path others had slavishly trodden before him. On the way home I realised how much he'd impressed Miss and I was deeply surprised. Infatuation had me in its prickly grasp and Charles P. Puddlejumper was here to stay.

Five

I met a holy man once who told me this story. Jesus had just raised a man from the dead and he was walking away from the empty tomb when an onlooker approached. The man fell to his knees in front of the Lord to block his path. 'Master, tell me the sacred words you used to draw life into the stinking corpse,' he begged. 'Reveal to me the mysteries of your blessings.'

'You don't understand what you're asking of me,' Jesus replied, dismissively. 'If you had any inkling of that terrible thing which you desire you wouldn't want me to tell you.'

'I beg you, master,' the man implored. 'Share your knowledge with me. I promise I will only employ the gift for good works and never for evil.'

Jesus looked into the man's heart and knew that his spirit was well-intentioned. He had a genuine desire to help others who were less fortunate than himself.

'Very well,' the Lord conceded with infinite compassion. 'But you must be careful to use this knowledge wisely.' Then he leaned in close to whisper the words so no one else would hear.

The grateful man was overjoyed. He tearfully took his leave of the master after kissing his hand many times. Then he set off towards his home, a village that had recently been ravaged by a terrible plague. It was a long journey along a dry, dusty desert-path.

Along the way he stopped to rest by the side of the road. While he was sitting in the shade of a date palm he noticed a scattering of sun-bleached bones that had been exposed by the shifting sands. He said to himself, 'I wonder if the master's words will really raise the dead. Here is a creature that has perished from starvation. This will be the perfect test.'

He leaned close over the lifeless remains and whispered. In an instant, before his disbelieving eyes, the shards of bone transformed themselves. Flesh and sinew knitted together; blood and muscle, tooth and claw took form; until a great emaciated lion sat before him. It was drooling at the sweet scent of fresh flesh.

The hungry beast roared in triumph. The man froze with fear. And before he could draw the knife from his belt the lion tore him into a thousand pieces.

As my tenth year of schooling ended it didn't look like I had much of a future ahead of me but I'd already begun a lifelong habit of optimism. Some might argue that my bright outlook wasn't really justified. They might even say that I was in denial of what lay ahead for me. All I cared about was enjoying what little freedom I had left to me. I didn't give the future too much thought. The only decision I'd made was not to continue school beyond tenth grade, the legal requirement. I couldn't see much point in wasting my days in that place.

Miss loaned me the *Tibetan Book of the Dead* and I devoured it with enthusiasm. Even though most of the esoteric symbolism went over my head the basic concepts seemed so much more reasonable than the Bible; especially the Book of Job. I mean, who'd want to bow down to a god who covers your body in boils just to test your loyalty? Not me or any other 16-year-old I've ever met.

On the other hand, reincarnation seemed to make perfect sense. The journey of the soul through trials and tribulations; learning all the way, progressing and improving, gradually opening one's spirit to the source of divine love. That's my style. It's certainly a much more positive outlook than a stark choice between the torments awaiting sinners in the eternal fires of Goodna or the everlasting joys reserved for the rapturous elect in Heaven.

Buddhism wasn't the only spiritual tradition I encountered that spoke of human souls as being splinters or shards of the divine spirit. Many holy men and women claimed that the purpose of life is to mend the splintering we all suffer from and to return in unity to the One. The precepts of Buddhism had a profound effect on my thinking.

It's obvious to me now why Christianity wasn't very appealing. Nevertheless, I was open-minded enough to give Jesus a try. One day a group of American evangelical missionaries visited our school. They were three fastidiously groomed men who called themselves the Fishers of Men. Everyone sat down in the middle of the sports ground and our impressionable minds were subjected to an hour of fire and brimstone in the sweltering summer heat.

I was soaked in sweat but I enjoyed the theatricality of the show, especially all the lurid talk about fornication and the evils of the communists who were all in the pay of Satan. The chief-preacher was a man in his 40s, slightly overweight with thick dark-rimmed glasses. He spoke of the Glorious Rapture; though in his exotic Texan drawl it sounded more like rupture to me.

Toward the end of the prayer meeting he summoned all those who were willing to invite Christ into their hearts to step forward and be blessed. I sat up and took notice when he promised God would heal his faithful servants of all their sins and right the terrible wrongs they had done. Now those sorts of words strike hope into the heart of anyone who believes that all the troubles of the world are his personal responsibility. I stood up like a shot out of a gun and shouted out.

'Will Jesus heal me?'

I'd taken the bait and now all the fisherman had to do was reel me in.

'Come down here son and let the Lord Jesus Christ work his will in your life!'

As I dodged through the crowd the Mahjee turned away from me in disgust. Charles P. Puddlejumper washed his hands of the whole affair and scoffed at my gullibility. But I wasn't going to be put off a golden opportunity to be free of the burden of my shame-dragon. By the time I reached the raised stage, I'd been abandoned by my two closest allies. The preacher asked me my name as he held the microphone up to my mouth.

I leaned close and paused a moment to take in the crowd as a wave of terror washed through me. I couldn't get my tongue to work. It was the longest moment of my life. At last I coughed and found I could speak.

'I'm Feeble,' I stuttered. The crowd tittered. I realised what I'd said. I thought I was going to faint.

The Texan covered the microphone with one hand, frowned with suspicion, and growled at me through gritted teeth, 'Are you shitting me, son?' He sounded like John Wayne getting worked up for a shoot-out. I shook my head. I didn't want to get in more trouble by admitting I'd let my madness get the better of me.

'My name's Chameleon Feeble.'

He squinted, tried to pronounce my first name then turned his attention back to the congregation, aware that he could lose them to the slightest distraction.

'O Lord Jesus!' he exclaimed, raising his eyes to Heaven with his free hand lifted high; fingers splayed wide. 'Look down this day on our dear brother Feeble, who has shown us what true courage can do. We ask You, Lord Jesus, to bless him this day with the divine glory of Your love. Grant him the grace of Your forgiveness, O Lord Jesus, and set a place for him at the feasting table where the Chosen Ones will gather on Judgement Day.'

Then he stepped around in front of me and did a most unexpected thing. He placed his free hand on my forehead and sternly looked me directly in the eyes. I reacted straightaway to this invasion of my personal space by moving back a little out of his reach. But every time I shuffled away he stepped closer until my heels were hanging over the rear edge of the stage and there was nowhere left for me to go. I struggled not to tumble backwards.

'Do you reject Satan and the powers of darkness?' he shouted into the microphone so that the speakers screeched with ear-splitting feedback.

'I do,' I stuttered nervously, aware perhaps I'd bitten off more than I could chew.

'Do you accept the Lord Jesus Christ into your heart? Do you proclaim the glorious advent of the Kingdom of Heaven for all eternity?'

'I do.'

'Do you renounce the sins of the flesh and all forms of fornication for all time?'

The audience oohed and aahed with amusement. There was widespread sniggering. Someone farted loudly.

'I do,' I replied tentatively.

I later wondered whether it was ethical to renounce something I was yet to experience. Before it crossed my mind that I'd probably perjure myself at some later date, two of the preacher's aides suddenly appeared at either side of me and grasped my elbows. I squirmed free of them, unwilling to be touched by strangers.

Then the Texan placed his palm hard against my forehead again and shouted, 'By the power of the Holy Spirit working through me and in the name of Our Lord Jesus Christ I bless you, brother Feeble.' The pressure increased as he paused, took a deep breath and yelled at the top of his voice, 'I heal you!'

With that he pushed me back hard. I was already on the very edge of the stage so I immediately lost my balance. As I teetered backwards his aides tried to grab me. I managed to push them away. It was only at the last instant before I fell that my survival instincts kicked in and I reached out to grab at anything that would stop me falling. I got hold of the preacher by the collar of his shirt.

Before he could fight me off I'd tumbled backwards dragging him, the two aides, the microphone and a hissing speaker box. The whole school cracked up and cheered. That was the end of the prayer meeting and my all-too-brief relationship with Jesus.

The preacher twisted his ankle badly and had to be taken away in an ambulance. As they strapped him down on the stretcher he told me off for disrupting his sermon. He said I'd be damned for what I'd done. In a final dramatic gesture he withdrew his blessing and the healing from me. With a straight face one of his aides quietly asked me if I was some kind of communist insurgent.

I was bitterly disappointed. I can laugh about it all now, but at the time I really thought I'd blown my chances with Jesus. I hadn't meant to damage one of his ministers. I couldn't help being bad. My heart was broken. I was deeply depressed and ashamed of myself. I'd come so close to being freed from my dragon. To have the opportunity snatched away when it was within my grasp was a shattering experience. To cap it off I received six of the best across the back of the hand.

Shortly after my brush with the evangelicals, I was passed over in the selection process for the Queen's Honour Guard during the Royal visit. I'd spent so much energy and time practising for that guard. I couldn't believe all my fellow cadets had been chosen and I'd been left out. I felt worthless. I found out two years later that Mother had contacted my commanding officer and told him I was on the waiting list for Goodna. He wouldn't have been doing his duty if he'd let a loony with a fixed bayonet get anywhere near the Queen.

The rejection was paralysing. I withdrew into myself and became even more of a loner at school, so it took a month or two for me to realise I'd become a bit of a folk hero among my peers. In the last week of school Miss kept me after class one afternoon. She told me she hoped I'd be returning the next year to finish high school.

Even though Feeble had already decided to give up school the Mahjee assured her I'd be back. It seemed to please her. She casually invited me to an end-of-year party at her house. She'd asked a select group of her favourite students and I was among them.

I thought she was pulling my leg, but I went along the next Saturday afternoon to her house. I was surprised to find that some of the cooler students in my year wanted to find out more about me. Charles P. and the Mahjee were in their element, but Feeble wasn't in a talking mood and I had to report to my cadet unit that evening so I made my excuses and left.

A few weeks later I was returning from a training exercise with my unit when I ran into Miss. She invited me back to her house to show me a book she'd found on meditation. The Mahjee snapped up the offer and Mr Puddlejumper was shivering with anticipation.

She ended up telling me about Pranic breathing techniques and we spent the day together talking, laughing and listening to music. It was after sunset when I realised I might be missed by Mother but by then I wasn't in a hurry to go home. Charles P. convinced me to stay on a while longer. As it turned out Mother didn't even notice I was missing and never asked where I'd been.

In the early evening a friend of Miss turned up. She was an Asian woman of about the same age as Miss and she was also a teacher. She had an educated English accent and she laughed all the time. I'd never spent time with an Asian person before. I was fascinated by her. She spoke of meditation techniques she'd learned in India and the spiritual journey she'd set off on when she was 18. The Mahjee was inspired. He wanted to know more. He asked her if she'd teach him a few things.

The two of them laughed at my naïveté and Miss set about rolling a joint, the first one I'd ever seen. Feeble was extremely frightened because the atmosphere was suddenly charged with an unfamiliar energy and he didn't understand what was going on. The Mahjee was quietly interested in this strange ritual. But it was Mr Puddlejumper who enthusiastically stepped to the fore as soon as he got an inkling there were rules about to be broken.

As I've already said, I was a chameleon. I just wanted to please everyone. It didn't take much peer pressure to push me over the edge. So I shared a smoke with them.

What I noticed immediately was that Feeble disintegrated completely as if he'd never been. All my chronic anxiety melted away. A weight was removed from my shoulder and I sat up straight. The shame-dragon was gone.

At the same time the autistic parts of me I'd suppressed for so long – the stuttering, the ticks and the weird word associations – were suddenly set free. My senses fired up more intensely than they'd ever done before, but instead of shutting down I was able to revel in the experience of being me.

In a short while I was laughing and enjoying myself with two people who accepted me for who I was and, what's more, seemed to like my company. The Mahjee, Charles P. and Feeble vanished back into one identifiable person. I was relaxed and calm in a way I'd never been before and all it took was one little puff of a strange-smelling herb.

You have to remember that this was the late seventies in Queensland. Back then this stuff grew everywhere. You could throw down a few seeds and they'd sprout up as if by magic in the rich volcanic soil south of Brisbane. The tropical climate and heavy rainfall in those days before the drought, ensured the plants needed no looking after whatsoever. It was not uncommon for a home to have a private garden where a hemp plant sprouted. And there were few, if any, dealers.

The stuff Miss grew was a world away from the nasty, super-strong hydroponic garbage they sell on the streets today. That modern rubbish is bred to produce maximum dependency and profit for the money-hungry drug dealers who peddle it. The intention behind it is evil and it spreads poisonous misery and addiction.

I don't believe the hard stuff that's around today is any good for anyone but, that said, cannabis isn't a black and white issue to me. At the time it had a profoundly positive effect on my life. The smallest amount was enough to calm me down and allow me to see everything in perspective. I didn't desire to have it every day or in any quantity. I wasn't hooked on it; it was just another interesting experience.

I've never been able to get addicted to anything, and believe me, I've tried. I prefer having my wits about me. And I'm too easily bored to seek out the same experiences over and over again; unless I develop an obsession. Fortunately drugs and alcohol have never fascinated me that much that I'd ever become obsessed with them.

I stayed the night at my teacher's house. Without going into all the details I'll just say that many things changed for me in that 24-hour period. Today she'd probably be in serious trouble for over-stepping the boundaries of the teacher–student relationship, but in those days such friendships were not taken quite so seriously as long as they were kept strictly private.

It could be argued that Miss took advantage of a troubled, vulnerable youth. That's probably true to some extent, and my experience with her certainly set the scene for other unbalanced relationships in the future. On the other hand, I doubt that I would have been exposed to meditation, spiritual practices or alternative viewpoints to my condition if it hadn't been for her.

Also she strictly controlled how much cannabis I had and watched over me with an experienced eye. She taught me that less is more when it comes to medication. The less I had, the more I felt comfortable. Once I got past a critical small dose my anxiety could take over again and send me into panic. But with the help of Miss I started to see what it was like to be at least partly normal. My stress, shame and anxiety were lifted sometimes for days afterwards.

Autism was as irrelevant to Miss and her friend as superficial racial differences were to me. Feeble was gradually reassured about these two women because they were comfortable with themselves, their places in the world and with sexuality.

I discovered that touch wasn't something I hated after all. It was an experience I revelled in and loved to explore; the same as I love all my other senses. What made touch unpleasant for me was the conditioning I'd been subjected to that left an expectation that touch must be accompanied by severe physical punishment and pain.

I'd never received much nurturing from Mother or family so I soaked up the whole experience with Miss. In time I was exposed to her wider circle of friends who also appeared to accept me. Indeed, a few of her friends became my first real human companions. I came to understand that I'd been forced by circumstance to become an isolated chameleon.

Miss was a very positive influence on me and I believe I was taken under her wing just in time to save me from a much worse fate. Within the next 12 months other drugs appeared in Brisbane. Heroin and LSD were everywhere and in the extremely bleak surroundings of that city these avenues for escape became very popular. Due entirely to the influence of Miss I never dabbled in either of these two substances.

By the end of 12th grade I knew of three students who'd died from heroin. I watched otherwise intelligent and promising young people fall to its dark allure. It was as if they'd had their souls stolen. To my horror I recognised something about heroin addicts. They appeared very similar to me when I was shut down. They were zombies.

An acquaintance in the cadets had a girlfriend who was on prescription medication for depression. To me she didn't appear to be that much different from the heroin zombies I knew. When she was taken off her medication for a short while she took up heroin. She was dead within six months.

At my senior formal I witnessed a young man completely losing his mind on LSD. He was taken straight to Goodna where he remained imprisoned without review for years. I vowed never to take anything that had the potential to do that to me. I felt I was much more at risk than 'normal' people. These experiences frightened me enough to work hard at meditation as an alternative to medication.

The Mahjee took on the role of protector in this regard. Whenever a situation arose where there was peer pressure to take drugs, he quickly withdrew me from the danger so Chameleon Feeble wouldn't succumb.

Puddlejumper on the other hand didn't like to mollycoddle Feeble, so he was always in conflict with the Mahjee and consequently getting me into trouble. My life became a bitter struggle between these two aspects of my personality. One day Charles P. might have the upper hand, the next it was the Mahjee. Chameleon Feeble could only sit back and watch them play out their chess game, each trying to gain the initiative over the other.

In 11th and 12th grade I continued an affair with Miss that we managed to keep secret from everyone in our immediate day-to-day environment. Her close friends knew all about it, but my parents never guessed because they didn't care what I got up to.

I'd skip parades at cadets. I'd lost interest after my duties were cut back and my application for the naval reserve was rejected. Instead of going to the navy base I'd turn up at my teacher's house and we'd spend the weekend together. I was introduced to the complex music and the intricate poetic lyrics of bands like Jethro Tull and Pink Floyd, and virtuoso musicians such as Ravi Shankar.

My meditation practice intensified over time to the point where I felt the need to make it a daily part of my life in order to explore the potential of the experience. I'd sit three or more hours a day in absolute silence when the rest of the house was asleep, and this soon raised me to a new level of awareness about myself. I was determined to unravel the mystery of myself, to find out what made me tick.

I began to notice that whenever I'm overwhelmed the first sign is a gentle rocking that can sometimes escalate into a rhythmic seated dance. To begin with I thought I had to suppress this urge to rock back and forth. I saw it as a negative manifestation of autism. After a year battling against the urge to rock in my seat and to tap out rhythms with my fingers, feet and hands, I finally gave up the fight.

It wasn't until I allowed my body to drum itself into a deeper relaxation that I started to get real results from meditation exercises. Rhythm profoundly calmed my over-stimulated senses and released the tension of my pent-up emotions.

With the encouragement of Miss I took up the drum. She introduced me to a fellow who'd spent time in Iran studying with the Dervishes. I became interested in the timeless Sufi tradition of dancing in order to reach a state of ecstatic trance.

Her friend was surprised how remarkably easy it was for me to achieve trance. He'd been studying for years and he still found it difficult. My ease with trance is one of the most positive outcomes I can point to that developed from the traumatic circumstances of my childhood. Puddlejumper would have said, 'The dunny turned out to be lined with silver.'

I discovered that rhythm works for me on several levels. Tapping the keyboard when I write a book or my blog is exceptionally soothing. I access a deep creative trance using this method.

At the end of 12th grade I'd decided I wanted to study at university. The trouble was my results weren't nearly good enough. So I put in a request to repeat my final year. Mother didn't care what I did. As far as she was concerned I wouldn't be around much longer so it didn't really matter what I did to fill in time. She reckoned at least this way I wasn't going to be hanging around the house all day.

I went back to school and found it much easier to socialise. It still wasn't as easy for me to fit in, but Miss, the Mahjee and Mr Puddlejumper were of invaluable support. I can look back now and understand I wasn't ready to set out on my own. I'd become dependent on Miss for my self-esteem and a sense of safety. She realised this and very wisely began to cut the strings between us.

I resigned from cadets when I was passed over for promotion on account of my autism and obvious anxiety. That was the end of my military aspirations. I began hanging out with people I'd met through Miss. For the first time I was able to choose my own subjects at school. I took art and music as well as English and history.

Sadly, my music teacher was a snob who told me I was wasting my time in his class because I was retarded. He refused to teach me unless I could read and write musical notation. So I learned nothing from him. He was an accomplished jazz musician, but he came across as an elitist insecure poseur. The best thing about him was that he let me sleep at the back of the room.

Art, on the other hand, was very interesting. My teacher didn't think much of me though. She was another bloody-minded snob who questioned my motives for entering her class and warned me not to expect any special treatment. I sat back and listened to everything she had to say. I learned how to use a 35mm camera and develop my own film. My fascination with surrealism, expressionist theatre and dada began.

The end-of-year assignment was a self-portrait. I painted myself as a strange-looking tree-creature with one teary eye and gum leaves shaped like toothy smiling mouths. There was a lightning bolt touching one of the gum leaves as it burst into flame. The teacher completely freaked out when I handed it in. Poor woman. Her head was so stuck in Queensland she simply couldn't cope. She must have stared at it dumbfounded for almost ten minutes. Sadly, she just didn't get what I was on about at all.

I started wandering around with a cardboard smile on a stick which I'd hold up to my mouth whenever anyone approached me. My art teacher thought I was mocking her. I officially failed art class for being too surreal. So it didn't turn out too bad, after all.

While I was adventurous with my artistic expression I was also oblivious of most people around me. They simply didn't interest me at all. I was shocked and frightened when a girl I hardly knew threw herself on me one morning before school and groped me. I was comfortable with physical boundaries being breached by people I knew well, but everyone else had to stand back. I challenged my fear of parties by accepting every invitation. At parties I could allow my guard down as an experiment and know I could safely retreat without too much harm being done.

The Asian friend of Miss returned after a long while in India. She and I became very good friends. I called her Tantrika because she'd been studying under a Tantric practitioner – known in India as a *tantrika* – and she was deeply involved in those ancient practices.

Tantra yoga in the West is almost completely focused on sex and sexual practices. In India it is a purely spiritual tradition, the focus of which is spiritual growth through meditation, physical yoga practice and self-discipline. An approach to sex is a very small part of that tradition. However, especially in the last 20 years, Tantra has become synonymous with sex in Western countries.

Tantrika was more interested in the Indian tradition. But she also taught me a lot about meditation and helped me to explore touch, love-making and sexuality in a safe setting where I wasn't feeling hemmed in or frightened. I suppose to some extent, as a good-looking, innocent young man, I was being exploited and this has been pointed out to me before. It doesn't really matter to me.

If I hadn't been exposed to the influences of Tantrika and Miss I wouldn't be the independent person I am today. I certainly wouldn't have had the confidence or the incentive to broaden my horizons.

The Mahjee dominated my life at that time. He was a sober individual who sincerely wanted to do good works. He recognised that he had to learn skills if he was going to survive in the real world. By the end of my repeated 12th year of school my results weren't that much better than before. I'd tried studying harder and dedicated myself to my work but it didn't seem to make any difference. I sat a new intelligence test and got the lowest possible score.

I now know that I have to be deeply interested in a subject if I'm going to excel at it. I can write a novel in four months if I'm totally lost in the world of the story and inspired by the characters. If I'm forced to write an article under a contractual obligation I'm far less likely to do a good job of it. I have to be passionate about the means to have any hope of achieving the end.

My school results had improved but I'm a harsh judge of myself. I'd scored enough to get into university but I still gave myself a hard time and told everyone I'd done badly. At the same time Miss was making her break with me as gently as she could. She realised I was going to be placed in hospital soon and probably medicated. She didn't believe there was anything that could be done about the situation and she was trying to make it easy on both of us. Tantrika returned to her family in Hong Kong.

School ended and I was left with no direction in life. My parents were set against me enrolling in university. I was the first member of my family to finish school to 12th grade. University students were looked on with suspicion by mainstream Australia at that time because the anti-war movement had been championed by students.

Father was renovating the house that summer. I'll never forget the look on his face when he excavated a wall under the house and out tumbled 30 rolling pins. He didn't know what was going on. I'd almost forgotten about my hiding place.

Mother was livid. She called me every name under the sun. Father picked one of the pins up to hit me but I was too quick for him. By then I'd been bullied enough to know how to look after myself.

I easily disarmed him, tossed the rolling pin at Mother and pushed him away. Father rushed back at me with his fist raised ready to strike. Before he had a chance to hit me I punched him hard in the jaw and knocked him flat. It was so quick I hardly knew what had happened. There was no rage involved. I just did it.

My blood turned to ice. I thought I'd killed him. He lay there motionless on his back while Mother went on screaming that I was a little bastard and that I'd murdered my old man. Outside I heard a siren wailing and I swallowed hard. I went to the window and saw a fire-engine passing by on the top road.

Mother threw some cold water over Father and he stirred. I was relieved I hadn't killed him but I felt terribly guilty. I realised I'd resorted to the same tactics as my parents. I'd used violence. I knew I'd had a hard time but I didn't want to turn out just as bad as them. I vowed I'd never do that to anyone again, and I'm proud to say that from that day to this, I haven't.

Mother got her revenge on me for the rolling pins. She wasn't the kind to let anyone get the better of her. I came home one afternoon to find all my books had been placed on the bonfire. She waited until I was watching before she threw the skin of the green tree-man on to the flames. He burned and she laughed, but I never let on how much that dried-up old snakeskin meant to me.

Her destructive act inspired me to go against their wishes and enrol in university. It was a waste of time. Father soon put a stop to that. He turned up at the registrar and, through his Masonic connections, had me struck off. I sank into depression while the Mahjee tried to work out exactly what had gone wrong. A short while later I contracted bronchitis.

A wise person once said: There are two kinds of people in this world – those who categorise folks into two distinct types and those who don't.

Father was a bigot. To his way of thinking there was one type of person in the world. They were white-skinned, intelligent, athletic and, most important of all, they were normal. No one else counted as human. I wasn't normal, so I was classed as one of the non-people.

Father took me to a doctor who gave me a thorough medical examination. He told me I had a severe hernia which would need to be operated on as soon as possible. A date was booked for the operation.

When I'd recovered from the bronchitis I was sent away on a short holiday to stay with distant cousins in the far south of Australia. While I was there I was warned that it was my parents' plan to have me sterilised and placed in a home for the mentally ill. My cousin's husband in particular didn't agree with what my parents were doing and urged me to try to escape.

I went to a doctor in Melbourne who couldn't find any evidence of a hernia. That placed me in a very difficult position. While I was sure I'd end up in care eventually, I'd also grown quite used to being free of restrictions. The Mahjee wasn't ready to give up his freedom just yet and Puddlejumper was angry at being pushed around.

I came to the conclusion that I had no choice but to escape. The Mahjee stepped in and organised everything. He arranged for me to go on the dole and lined up accommodation for me. He then set about getting a job because he'd decided he wanted to go to India and follow the life of the spirit. Tantrika had inspired me.

It was one of the few occasions when he and Charles P. Puddlejumper agreed on anything. However, Charles P. had no real interest in India. He wanted to go to England, the home of Monty Python, Jethro Tull and the Holy Grail.

When I returned home, all my meagre possessions had been packed into boxes. I took a few clothes and books and a few days later, without any fanfare, I quietly moved into my new home. It was a room in a house that was being rented by an acquaintance from school. Within a month I'd started work as a filing clerk at a local shire council.

My parents didn't make any attempt to track me down. I was suddenly free. Over the first six months after I moved out I had some hard lessons. Miss was transferred to North Queensland, a thousand kilometres away. We lost contact.

The people I shared the house with discovered that I kept all my pay in cash in my closet. I didn't understand about bank accounts at that time. They pilfered my money bit by bit. I never noticed because I've never been interested in money except as a means to an end.

A woman from work asked me to move in with her so without a thought for the consequences, I did. Life got easier and within a year I'd almost saved up enough money for my flight. I'd been having a sexual relationship with the woman I'd moved in with and she was devastated that I wanted to go overseas. I'd been so focused on my desire to travel that I'd hardly noticed when she seduced me to her bed. I suppose that sounds heartless, but I simply didn't understand what those sorts of relationship were supposed to mean. At that time I hardly had any clue about life. I may have been well-read and spiritual but I had very little life experience.

It was a pattern I'd see repeated again and again throughout my journey. I think the trouble came from wanting and enjoying physical intimacy yet having been punished for initiating it in the past. The sense of touch is bound up with guilt so closely it's hard for me to disentangle them one from the other. In later years whenever physical contact was initiated by another person I'd be fine and I'd usually surrender to the moment. But at that time I was still shutting down into Chameleon mode and therefore vulnerable to being led along paths that I probably would have preferred not to walk.

Puddlejumper had allowed the sexual relationship to develop against the Mahjee's wishes. Chameleon Feeble just wanted to make everyone happy so he'd gone along with whatever she wanted to do. In her bitterness at my determination to leave, this woman arranged for me to lose my job, just short of my goal of four thousand dollars.

The Mahjee quickly found another place to stay across town in a shared house with two university students. For six months I slaved as a filing clerk at the university. I bought a motorcycle so I could travel to work and learned all about the engine by stripping it down and putting it back together again over and over. The Mahjee was my constant companion. He kept me very busy and he rarely let the disruptive Puddlejumper out to play.

I got a second job reading the weather at a left-wing radio station on the university campus, and through that job I became interested in alternative views of the world. I marched in demonstrations for native land rights and became very good friends with my two flatmates who were political activists.

They were a strange pair. I remember thinking at the time that they were quite interesting women but they seemed to hate men so much. I'd connected with them from the moment we met. We remained close friends until one of them made an attempt to consummate the friendship. I put it down to too much rum and the Mahjee tersely nipped it in the bud.

Things got uncomfortable at home after that so I started looking for excuses to stay out. I met a group of Krishna devotees who invited me to hang out at the temple in Brisbane. I ended up spending quite a lot of time with them. I learned about their spiritual practices and helped to prepare the wonderful vegetarian food they were famous for.

I read the *Bhagavad-Gita* for the first time. This ancient Vedic text challenged me to see my life through different eyes. The *Gita* is one part of the epic poem known as the *Mahabharata*. The story is about Arjuna the archer, and his charioteer, Krishna. They come to Kurukshetra to fight the opening battle in a terrible war. Arjuna expresses doubts about whether he wants to be part of this conflict. His cousins are in the opposing army and he doesn't want to be responsible for their deaths. This gives Krishna the opportunity to explain that the material world is an illusion and that there is no such thing as death. Krishna encourages Arjuna to do what he was born to do – to fight as a warrior and passionately play his part in the great drama of life without allowing fear to get the better of him. Krishna then reveals himself as the eternal supreme being who has brought all things into existence. According to Krishna, standing back from life and failing to become involved with the world is just as detrimental to the spirit as extreme indulgence. There was one verse that struck me in particular:

The humble sage, by virtue of true knowledge, sees with equal vision a learned and gentle brahmana, a cow, an elephant, a dog and a dog-eater (an outcaste).
(*Bhagavad-Gita As It Is*, chapter 5, verse 18, translated by
His Divine Grace Bhaktivedanta Swami Prabhupada)

That verse moved me to tears. When I read it I understood that I held the same divine spark within me as every other living thing on this planet. I glimpsed the possibility that I wasn't as worthless as I had been taught. The *Gita* got me thinking that perhaps my life was a blessing after all and that I should live it to the full even though I might be retarded and less-than-human.

Father's sister, Auntie, had impressed upon me her view that I was inhabited by a demon and that God was punishing me with the affliction of autism. Unless I repented, she'd warned me, I'd be stained with sin for eternity. By the time I left home I realised I'd been autistic since I was very young. I asked myself – how could a little child have been so evil that God would want to punish him this severely? My family had been taken away from me. I was alone in the world. I was retarded and naïve. I was a target of ridicule and theft. And I would likely spend much of my life as a prisoner of the hospital system.

Why would such a god pinpoint small children as targets for his wrath yet overlook the lies of politicians who were responsible for the deaths of so many? The more I heard Christians speaking about their God, the less I liked the way He operated. I went to a few churches to try to reconcile this and I was shocked to hear preachers speaking about native Australians as inhuman or homosexuals as servants of evil.

I didn't question that autism was a kind of punishment back then. I hadn't yet come to appreciate it as a gift. Feeble was confused and he thought about going to a psychologist, but the Mahjee always calmed him down and talked him out of it. Then one day I bumped into Mother in the city.

She told me my place had finally come up in the mental hospital and the police were looking for me. She'd signed the papers committing me into care at the discretion of the government chief medical officer. She advised me to hand myself in.

Feeble was terrified. He wanted to do the right thing but the Mahjee and Puddlejumper weren't ready to surrender. That night they fought it out as I wandered aimlessly around the backstreets of Brisbane. I ended up sitting in Musgrave Park with a group of Aboriginals. They were drinking heavily and Charles P. decided to join them. I laughed a lot that night and got myself very drunk.

Next morning I awoke under a tree and had a terrible vision of what might happen to me. I knew the police would track me down eventually and, whether I had a steady job or not, they'd put me away. In fact they were more likely to track me down through my employer. I realised I was doomed to a life on the streets unless I headed overseas.

The Mahjee got me home in time to shower and dress for work. All the way he was telling me it was time to leave. Move on, he said over and over. Move on while you still can.

Later I was riding my motorcycle to work when some idiot in a Volvo cut me up and nearly killed me. I pulled up beside him at the next set of traffic lights, got off my bike and told him what I thought of him. He sat tight behind his tinted windows and didn't respond. That really annoyed me so I kicked his door a few times then rode off. When I got to work I discovered it had been my boss. He sacked me on the spot.

That afternoon I sold the bike to someone I knew and found I had just over four thousand dollars saved. The Mahjee pressed that it was time to go before things got out of hand. I'd already got my passport organised so I bought an airline ticket to Thailand.

A week later on the plane to Bangkok I had plenty to think about. I'd escaped by the skin of my teeth. I was determined to make the best of my life while it was still mine to make the best of. I'd renounced family, possessions, friends, employment and home. Quite by accident, rather than design, my journey had taken on the attributes of a sacred pilgrimage.

After I'd spent some time in Thailand I moved on to India where the Mahjee led me from one adventure to another. I was robbed of my passport and ended up staying with devotees of Krishna at their temple in Delhi. While I waited for new documents I learned all I could about Ayurvedic cooking. I became a confirmed vegetarian.

In typical fashion I committed hundreds of precise recipes to memory. Other skills I'd learned in the past were dumped off the hard drive in my head to accommodate this new obsession. For example, I forgot how to speak French. I can still understand the language to this day but I can't put a sentence together. I placed all I'd soaked up about motorcycle mechanics in the trash leaving only the basics with which to get by.

I travelled to Vrindavan, where the devotees had a temple, and then on to Agra where I was introduced to a *tantrika*. I stayed with her in her house for ten months studying meditation practices before I was led by the Mahjee to travel further afield in India seeking holy people. I met sadhus who had renounced the material world to wander about the country near-naked. They wore their hair in dreadlocks called *jatta*.

In India the concept of holy is quite different from that we have in the West. Many of the most famous holy men and women would probably be considered stark raving loonies in Western terms. They live their lives in solitude on the fringes of society, mostly in quiet devotion to their chosen deity or in the earnest search for enlightenment.

Sadhus are venerated because of their commitment to the path and the gifts that set them apart from others. Today there are between four and five million wandering sadhus in India. When the Mahjee saw the sadhus he wanted to be just like them.

I lost a lot of time shut down in shock while I was on my great pilgrimage. I'd left home because there was no one I could rely on to stand up for me. This left me with a legacy of loneliness that lasted until quite recently.

After falling very ill with dysentery I eventually journeyed to Europe through Denmark and West Germany. I learned to speak German very quickly. It's not too different from English really. I stayed on an alp in Switzerland and practised the art of Gruyère cheese-making under the tutelage of a master.

Someone gave me an ounce of tobacco and some cigarette papers. I started compulsively rolling cigarettes with one hand as my grandfather had done. It was like a nervous twitch. Once I began rolling I simply couldn't stop myself. I must have had a hundred crammed into an old cigar box before I actually took up smoking them. I didn't particularly enjoy tobacco. I just had to get rid of the cigarettes somehow.

My money was thinning out so I thought I'd head back to India via the Khyber Pass. I made it to Turkey just as the borders to Afghanistan closed because of the Soviet occupation. So I turned around and headed back for London.

The Mahjee was very reluctant to go to England. He suspected that Puddlejumper would get himself in terrible trouble if he was allowed to run amok there. But there was little choice. I could have flown back to Australia after nearly two years on the road, but I knew I would have faced a bleak future. In England I'd be able to work legally and replenish my pilgrimage fund.

All the way to London the Mahjee and Charles P. were at loggerheads about what to do. I tarried in Berlin. I wandered aimlessly around the Rhine Valley and found a job picking grapes for a while. I was adopted by a German girl who invited me to stay with her near the Swiss frontier.

The Mahjee and Puddlejumper were fighting it out between them every step of the way. Charles P. was determined to get to London no matter what the cost. At last he resorted to desperate measures. I fell very ill. I was bleeding through my urinary tract. It got so bad I decided to go to London where I could claim a working holiday visa and get free medical treatment. As soon as I arrived the bleeding stopped and my health improved. Mr Puddlejumper had achieved his goal.

Charles P. loved London. He walked the streets until he knew parts of it like the back of his hand. He still does. I stayed in London a month before I found a good room in a house with five English people. The Mahjee landed me a job in a pub and began rebuilding my finances and consolidating all that I'd learned.

I was introduced to a couple of dreadlocked Rastafarians through an acquaintance. They were a wonderful down-to-earth couple who welcomed me into their lives without batting an eyelid. They took me to hear Rastafari poets like the mystic Benjamin Zefaniah. That man could improvise all night long about life on the cold, wet streets of Babylon-London. I longed to be able to scat like that. This was before American commercialised rap (with a silent 'C') tainted the music scene.

Inspired by my Rasta friends I wrote some of my own poems down, but I didn't like anything I'd composed. I concluded that the missing link in my poetry was the extremely potent ganja they were always smoking. The trouble was I couldn't stay awake long enough after partaking of their holy herb to come up with anything but silly drivel.

Worse than that, it seemed to block my dreams and atrophy my creativity. I drifted away from my Rasta friends as I started working double shifts and eventually lost contact with them altogether. In all the time I knew them it never crossed my mind that my fine golden strands of hair could be knotted into locks like theirs.

One cold autumn day after the Mahjee had his cup of chai at the Hare Krishna restaurant near Soho Square, Puddlejumper led me up to old Carnaby Street. I trawled the shops looking for unusual clothes as it was my wont to do.

A strange impulse led me to an ex-Royal Marines dress-uniform jacket. It was navy blue, adorned in reds and yellows about the collar and cuffs and sporting large, shiny brass buttons. It fitted perfectly and it only cost me ten quid. I joyously wore that jacket as I walked up towards one of my favourite people-watching haunts: Oxford Circus. Charles P. took up a position where I could observe the crowds.

That's when it happened. I experienced one of those miracle moments that have changed my life. From out of nowhere among the press of tourists and weary workers on their way home, a woman appeared. She was rushing down Oxford Street headed west, dressed in a long black coat, high black boots and white face make-up. I suppose she must have been some sort of proto-Goth, at the leading edge of dark-wave.

Her clothes were unusual for those days, but the thing about her that got my attention was her long honey-coloured hair. It flowed over her shoulders and halfway down her back in a cascade of knotted locks that took my breath away. I was so dumbstruck I didn't think to follow after her to get a better look, much less to ask her how a whitey had come to be wearing dreadlocks.

The Mahjee was gripped by epiphany. I'd seen locked hair on the Sadhus in India and the Mahjee had been so drawn to the renounced life he'd almost taken it up. As the dreaddie-woman crossed Regent Street against the traffic lights and vanished into the throng I knew with absolute certainty I could no longer suppress the outward manifestation of my true inner self – my eccentricity.

I saw dreadlocks as a path to freedom from the constraints of banal material culture, a rejection of standard notions of beauty. In my under-standing the dreadlock woman was laughing in the face of all the fashion fascists. I yearned to be like her one day. The Mahjee made me promise him that I'd lock my hair before they put me away in the mental hospital.

After that I relaxed a lot more about being eccentric. I noticed that the English were very accepting of eccentricity and that it was quite a common trait among them. A brief glimpse of a dreaddie-woman may not sound like a typically mystical experience, but I was completely trans-formed and the Mahjee was inspired.

From that time on, whenever I see myself in my dreams, I'm usually wearing long, knotted strands of golden hair. It goes without saying that the Mahjee identifies very strongly with locked hair.

Shortly after that experience I was introduced to the drug known as Speed. I'd never heard of it before. But then again I'd never met anyone who was openly homosexual until I went to London. I'd never heard of Rastafarians, Mods or Punks either. I took Speed for a while because it got me through two jobs in a six-day week but I didn't like the damage it did to my body so I cut it out and quit one of my jobs. The Mahjee quickly concluded that Speed didn't promote a spiritual life.

I was waking up to the fact that my journey was indeed a sacred pilgrimage and that I was opening myself to a new refreshed way of viewing my existence. In the back of my mind I was still very concerned about what people thought of me because I didn't want to be suddenly placed in care. I didn't want to be found out.

I stopped telling people about my autism altogether. This was a major step forward for me because I no longer felt obliged to live up to the definition of myself that had been foisted upon me by others. That decision also probably encouraged a new aspect of myself to make a split from the Mahjee and Puddlejumper. In the summer of my 22nd year, the Pilgrim emerged. He was a very adventurous part of me who also loved museums, storytelling and music. He shared a passion with the others for eccentric clothes so they grudgingly accepted him and made room.

To go to Rome is little profit, endless pain. The master you seek in Rome,
You find at home or seek in vain.

(Old Irish proverb)

I went off in search of healing, peace and, rather naively, a spiritual master who would help me be a better person. So much happened to me during the five years I was on pilgrimage that the story is deserving of a book in its own right. Perhaps I'll get around to telling that great tale with all its incredible coincidences one day. For now I'll just let you in on a few of the miracles that graced my pilgrimage.

I met a young Irish lad who inspired me to travel over the sea to the land of my forebears. I ended up staying in Ireland longer than intended. I learned to play the tin whistle and quickly picked up Gaelic. I was soon fluent enough to be able to start collecting traditional stories and songs from old folks in the Gaeltacht. I scribbled them all down in English along with sketches and poems. I had a thick journal that I kept close by my side for many years.

I met one old man who lived in a lighthouse on the west coast. He was all alone in the world and he preferred it that way. He was quirky and completely caught up in his own strange existence, but he was a magnificent storyteller. I listened to him tell tales all day long for six days and he never repeated himself once.

Unlike some storytellers he didn't mind me being around. He was going to be telling stories anyway. He spent every waking moment of his life reciting tales whether he had an audience or not. His fear of forgetting them was so great he felt compelled to run through them over and over even when he was alone walking the wild coastline gathering seaweed.

I'd just left his lighthouse when I had one of the most magical experiences of my life. I'd taken a shortcut down a lane that should have cut an hour off my journey to the main road. The signposts in Ireland weren't all that reliable in those days and I ended up walking all day.

It was a couple of hours before sunset when I met a farmer repairing a dry-stone wall. I wished him good day in Gaelic and he offered a blessing in return. Then unprompted he pointed up to the hill above us and said in English, 'You've arrived just in time.'

'What for?'

'Go and see for yourself.'

I put my pack down by the wall and climbed the hill. As I got near to the top I heard the wild cawing of many birds. Suddenly one bird screeched above the din of the others and they all fell silent. Then a strange sight was slowly revealed to me. I'll never forget it.

There was an oak tree; it wasn't very old, and it was full of ravens. There must have been a hundred of them perched on the branches and standing all around the base of the tree. At the very top in the highest parts there was a big old bird. I got the feeling it was a female: a queen. When I appeared all the birds broke out in a wild chorus of cries, caws and screeches. The noise was deafening. I had to put my hands over my ears. That went on for a few minutes until the queen threw back her head and raised her voice again. All the birds were instantly quiet.

I observed them for a while going through this strange pattern of cawing then silence before I went back down the hill to find the farmer. 'The raven-court doesn't meet too frequently these days,' he told me. 'I haven't seen it since I was a lad.' I was so impressed by that sight I worked the scene into my first novel and I've dreamed about those birds ever since.

I undertook sacred pilgrimages in Ireland and it was during one of those holy Christianised pagan journeys that I heard about the terrible conflict taking place in El Salvador. The Pilgrim returned to London intent on volunteering to help in whatever way he could. The El Salvador embassy told me to come back when I'd learned to speak Spanish. So I packed up and went off to Spain.

After a long journey by train from London to Malaga the Pilgrim ended up in a youth hostel in a small town in Andalusia. There were a number of other misfits there just like me. To my dying day I will never forget that wonderful place of sanctuary. Until the last few years those were the happiest days of my life. I felt truly loved, accepted and cared for while I was staying in the hostel.

I'm sure this was in no small part due to the warm, generous nature of the Spanish people. That hostel felt like home to me, in the same way my wife Helen feels like home to me now. The staff were a family of equals; each was respected for his or her part in the workings of the place. And at their head was the Colonel who was a retired officer in the Guardia Civil. During the Franco years the Guardia Civil were feared and hated for rounding up political dissidents. His family lived in the main house.

The youth hostel had been a convent before the civil war. The anarchists had cleared the nuns out and barricaded themselves within the walls. There they'd fought Franco's troops to the end in a bitter struggle that had cost many lives.

I was told that's why the government had put a retired Colonel in charge of the hostel. Up to then I'd heard a lot about fascists but until I met one I really had no idea what to expect. Make no mistake about it, the Colonel was a dyed-in-the-wool fascist who wore his uniform with pride. But he was also one of the few people who have ever completely accepted me for who I am.

The reason was simple. The Colonel had a son who was physically disabled and autistic. I nicknamed the Colonel's son Cristóbal Colón; the

Spanish rendering of Christopher Columbus. He called me Marco Polo, and we were great friends from the moment we met. The new part of me, the Pilgrim, immediately adopted the nickname Marco Polo. I liked the ring of it.

Within a few days of my arrival the Colonel spotted me talking with his son. He asked me into his office and quizzed me about my intentions in Spain; like the true military policeman he was. It was at that time he must have realised I was traumatised because I swapped between the Mahjee and Chameleon Feeble with such fluidity. I was fairly direct too, so he probably realised that I was autistic. He offered me a job at the youth hostel even though my visa specifically prohibited me from working in Spain. I was put to work in the gardens and given three months to learn some basic Spanish so I could act as his translator. In return I was given a place to sleep and three square meals a day.

Though the Colonel and his wife were pro-fascist the rest of the workers at the hostel had communist or anarchist sympathies. The Franco regime had only ended ten years earlier and the healing process was just beginning.

They all played a wonderful game with one another that I'll never forget. Every morning he put on an immaculate dark-green fascist uniform with polished black jack-boots and a shiny black leather *tricornio* – a three-cornered hat. At 8a.m. the Colonel would march out and stand before the flag pole. While his wife or eldest son ran the fascist flag up he'd salute proudly. When the ceremony was done he'd march back to his door, remove his hat, mop his balding head with a white handkerchief, then disappear inside. He reminded me of the Gestapo officer in the Humphrey Bogart film *Casablanca*.

The moment the Colonel and his wife closed the door to their house two of the hostel staff would make their way out from the adjoining kitchen. The old gardener would haul down the fascist flag and, without any ceremony at all he'd run the republican flag up the pole. Then he and his assistant would respectfully fold the Colonel's flag and place it on a wicker chair beside the front door.

That was typical of the way everyone used to put their differences aside and get on with life. It was so inspiring to live among these wonderful people. They took such good care of me. They asked me about the scar over my eye. They made sure I was fed and happy. The old gardener used

to take me out for coffee or a beer at siesta. I always had plenty of cigarettes, even though I didn't smoke a lot in those days.

I was speaking Spanish in three weeks. In six weeks I was so fluent the
Colonel used to ask me into his office every morning for half an hour to
ask me questions about Australia. I was soon being required to translate
from German to Spanish. Cristóbal picked up some German from me,
which made his father very proud. After that I was given a bottle of wine
every day as part of my pay.

Cristóbal used to stoop and had great trouble walking. His hands
were curled up tightly and his speech was slurred. He couldn't hold his
head still or look me in the eye but he was a wonderfully witty man.

In my first month at the hostel I heard an American couple speaking
about him. They'd hastily come to the unjust assumption he was slow-
witted and probably stupid as well. To his face they mocked him merci-
lessly, perhaps believing he couldn't understand them. He laughed and
laughed like a loon whenever they poked fun at him. At last, just as they
were leaving, Cristóbal grabbed the woman by the sleeve and said in
perfect English, 'You're very beautiful.'

She was so taken aback she could barely stutter a thank you.

'What a pity you're so ignorant,' he sighed. 'Fortunately, ignorance
can be cured. I will always be ugly.'

To me it was obvious Cristóbal was extremely intelligent and sharp-
witted. I immediately understood his point: that prejudice springs entirely
from ignorance. This incident also woke me up to the extent to which I'd
been subjected to prejudice throughout my life. As the old saying goes,
you're only ignorant of what you don't know. This realisation has been a
source of immense peace for me. Ever since that day, whenever I've been
persecuted for being different I've tried to feel compassion for the ignorance of those who've mistreated me.

Compassion has led me to be able to forgive others for something
they probably aren't even aware is one of their attributes – ignorance.
Don't get me wrong. I'm ignorant too. I'm just ignorant of different
things from you. I believe a degree of ignorance is one thing we all have
in common. When you look at it that way it's hard to stay angry with
anyone.

During siesta I used to go down to the waterfront and busk with my
tin whistle. I'd learned hundreds of traditional Irish and Scots melodies

by then but Marco Polo was tiring of the repertoire. Under his influence I began exploring free improvisation, which led to complex compositions that could stray on for half an hour or more and attract a large audience of Spanish people as well as tourists. These were my best money-spinners.

Soon afterwards Marco took up singing as well. I'd memorised many traditional songs while I was in Ireland. Out on the waterfront in Spain my voice became stronger each day and my range improved. The gardener took me to hear flamenco singers one afternoon and I decided that no matter what else happened in my life I would be a great singer.

Four months into my stay Marco Polo suddenly got itchy feet. He wanted some adventure. I hadn't had a bad lapse into trance since I'd been in Spain and Feeble was beginning to feel like he could stay there forever. The Mahjee warned against complacency. Puddlejumper was tired of the routine.

The three of them finally convinced Chameleon Feeble to go on a short trip to Gibraltar, further along the coast. Feeble couldn't see the harm in that so he agreed to it as long as it wasn't going to stretch the budget. Marco Polo promised to hitch down the coast road to save money.

This was one of the first times in my life when the four of them got together and discussed their plans in a civilised manner. It was one of the few times they ever managed to reach any sort of agreement that didn't leave one of them feeling hard done by.

Perhaps because I'd been feeling safer than I'd ever done before I was finally facing some of the terrible things that happened to me as a child. Incidents I'd blocked out of my memory were coming back to me as awful nightmares. At times I was extremely agitated. The slightest noise could set me off. I was regularly visited by night terrors. I slept with a knife under my pillow, even though I had nothing in the world to be frightened of in that peaceful place.

I slept very lightly in the dormitory among all those other males. As I've said before, I don't get on well with many men. I don't trust them for the most part.

One night just before I headed off on my adventure I was stirred from sleep by a noise. Before I knew what was happening the Mahjee had grabbed the knife. He passed it to Marco Polo while Charles P. and Feeble vanished. In a flash Marco had knocked a stranger to the floor and had the knife at his throat.

I heard an Australian accent shouting as someone tried to pull me away. Suddenly I snapped out of it, dropped the knife and sat back on my bunk. The bloke I'd knocked over had been going through the pockets of the fellow in the bunk above me. I'd caught him in the act and scared the crap out of him in the process.

Next morning the Australian I'd caught thieving made a complaint that I'd come close to stabbing him. The Colonel confiscated my knife and told me he was deeply disappointed. I tried to explain myself but he wouldn't let me say a word.

At the time I thought he was very angry with me, but the old gardener told me the Colonel was a very compassionate man who had been working behind the scenes on my behalf to get me a special visa so I could stay indefinitely in Spain. Though I hadn't said too much about my family, the Colonel and his wife had been looking into adopting me into theirs.

What I didn't understand at the time was that I had very obvious symptoms of the trauma I'd suffered. It was plain to everyone that I wasn't right in the head. I mean to say, I'd split myself into four distinct parts and I was sleeping with a knife under my pillow. How strange is that?

Before I left for Gibraltar the Colonel made me promise I wouldn't be gone more than a week. He gave me 500 pesetas and got the old gardener to drop me near the coast road.

My first lift arrived almost immediately. It was a Guardia Civil patrol car. As soon as I got in the two officers asked me to tell them some stories about Australia. They drove me to the border with Gibraltar. It wasn't until later that evening when I was settling down to sleep in a pension in Gibraltar that I realised the Colonel had sent them.

Back then the island of Gibraltar was very British. There were bobbies walking around. It was very strange after living in Spain for three months and not speaking much English. Charles P. was getting homesick for London. After a few days he suddenly rebelled against the others and tried convincing Feeble that it was time to head back to England.

Marco Polo was furious. The Mahjee attempted to keep the peace but Puddlejumper was in no mood to be told what to do. He'd had enough of

Spain and he made it clear he'd cause trouble if the others didn't give in to him. Marco did his best to come to a compromise by promising to return to the hostel immediately.

Unfortunately Puddlejumper met a wild Swiss-French girl who was keen on getting drunk and bedded. I spent the best part of a day drinking with her and the best part of the night otherwise engaged. I don't remember much of what happened but I'm sure Feeble felt so trapped and frantic that he simply bowed out at some stage.

The next thing I knew it was the middle of the next day and I was standing on the bow of the ferry that crossed from Spain to North Africa. Feeble awoke from his shut-down absolutely frantic with fear. I couldn't work out how I'd got into this situation. I went through my pockets and was relieved to find my passport and money were safe. I also found I had a return ticket to Ceuta.

It was the first of many blanks I can recall suffering in my life. There may have been earlier ones but this was the first I can pin down. I just couldn't figure out what had happened. I was becoming quite upset, close to tears. I could see Gibraltar in the distance behind the ferry. I could see Morocco looming into view ahead. But I just couldn't piece the puzzle together.

The Swiss girl was suddenly there beside me. She asked me how I was feeling. She'd just been seasick and she looked terrible. Apparently we'd decided to go to Morocco on the spur of the moment. The Mahjee cursed Puddlejumper aloud. Marco Polo stepped in while they were arguing and took control.

As soon as the ferry got into port Marco booked a cheap room in a pension for the Swiss girl and me. We spent the rest of the day recovering from our wild binge in Gibraltar. She went out to get some bread and came back with hashish as well. That wiped out another two days.

The Mahjee was soon getting bored. The Swiss girl was intelligent and witty but she didn't like being without some form of mind-altering substance in her system. Puddlejumper on the other hand was having the time of his life. Feeble didn't like hashish and neither did Marco. In the end Charles P. was outnumbered.

Marco was the only one who could get his head together enough to get me out of that situation. He convinced the Swiss girl that Morocco was too dangerous for her and sent her off on the next ferry back to Spain. Then he headed for the frontier and the next part of his adventure.

I was messed up. I was headed into one of the most dangerous experiences of my life. And yet I'm certain I was being watched over. The incident with the *gitanos* on my way back from Morocco is only half the story of what happened on that trip. I struck trouble the very moment I left Spanish territory.

Six

My journey to Morocco actually began almost a year earlier in Calais. I'd taken the ship from Dover for a weekend in Paris. After I passed through customs and out on to the road I met a young man with his head under the hood of a beaten-up old Citroën. I saw him try to turn the engine over and heard no sound came out of it. I knew straight away what the problem was; the battery terminals. I offered my assistance. Once the terminals were clean the engine sparked into life and my new found friend was slapping me on the back offering to buy me a drink.

I've already said that in those days if someone was friendly to me they were also my friend. This Moroccan lad was so warm to me that I couldn't help feeling like we were the best of friends. I declined his offer of a drink but I accepted a lift to Paris. Along the way we talked and talked. He was a fascinating fellow.

We were halfway to our destination before he admitted he was a drug courier running hashish. He'd just been across to England with his latest shipment and he was on his way home through southern France to Spain and on to Morocco.

He dropped me off in Paris and left me to marvel at some of the fascinating people I'd met on my journeys. Then as it happened he was the first person I bumped into after I crossed the frontier into Morocco almost 12 months later.

He recognised me immediately. I knew his face but I couldn't place him straightaway. That's a problem I've always had. Before I understood what was happening I was on my way back to his family house in the busy medieval city of Tétouan. I was welcomed with open arms by all and given a room to myself.

Marco Polo was in his element. There was danger everywhere. The streets were narrow and ancient. The casbah was abuzz; the market square was full of brightly dressed dancers and musicians. It was like stepping backwards in time. I felt like Doctor Who stranded in a parallel universe.

The culture shock was so great that I hardly recall anything of my life in Morocco. From the stamps in my passport I later worked out I'd been there a month but it could just as easily have been a week or a year. Marco Polo took over completely because he fitted in to the way of life very smoothly.

I recall I was taken up to the hills to watch the long donkey trains come in loaded with hashish for the European market. I sat in a tea shop all day long sometimes, sipping mint tea and listening to the conversations in French and Arabic. I went on short pilgrimages to Rabat and Tangier. I was introduced to camels and the teachings of the Holy Qur'an.

It was an old man in a tea house in Tétouan who told me the story about Jesus and the sacred words for raising the dead. It comes from the Arabic tradition. The old storyteller was illiterate. He taught me the difference between wisdom and learning. The psychologists and doctors who'd dealt with me in my youth had all been to university. Yet I felt this simple man living in a mud house in North Africa was wiser than all of them put together.

I tried to leave Morocco several times. On each occasion I was talked out of it; made to feel guilty or convinced that I would offend the family if I left before they'd shown their gratitude. Eventually I had to insist and actually walk out the door with my few remaining belongings. There were tears for my departure and I was torn to be leaving people who'd taken such good care of me.

But the Mahjee had remembered his promise to be gone for only a few days. Puddlejumper was getting bored and Marco Polo was keen to kick on to his next destination. Unfortunately they all left it up to Chameleon Feeble to make the move. You already know what happened as a result.

By the time I returned to the hostel in Spain my six-month visa was almost due to expire. The Mahjee presented a radical plan to reinvent

myself. I realised that my view of myself had been tainted by the prejudice and small-mindedness of Mother and Father.

I came up with a way to get past this brainwashing by creating a new
identity for myself. I decided I'd choose a new name and a new history
that would reflect the person I wanted to be rather than the defective I'd
been led to believe I was. I spent a few days working away on paper constructing this new identity convinced it was the way forward.

The Mahjee was very keen to get the refurbishment of my spirit
happening as soon as possible. He pushed me to meditate and analyse
myself searching for faults that could be redressed during the reinvention
process. I was very close to taking the step of transforming myself from a
silkworm into a moth when I realised it wasn't enough simply to take on a
new identity.

If I was going to fix all the problems I had been led to believe I
suffered from I was going to have to lay the old me to rest. In the same
way the moth sheds the former vestiges of the silkworm and the chrysalis
I was going to have to discard all traces of the old me. I would have to be
transformed in mind, body and spirit. At that time in my life I had no idea
how I was going to achieve such a daunting goal.

I struggled with this problem for days, determined to take the step to
moth. In the end I had to concede the worm had to build a chrysalis first
and then retreat into a sleep somewhat similar to death. Puddlejumper
eventually lost patience with the process of change and took matters into
his own hands.

He met a German girl who insisted I stay in the female dormitory
with her. It was the off-season; the hostel was almost empty. No one
seemed to mind me being there. I felt much better sleeping amongst the
women than the men. Something about the German girl was very
familiar. I was fascinated by her. I finally worked out that what I recognised about her was trauma. She, like me, had been brutalised as a child.
All she wanted was someone around who was like her. I found her
company very reassuring.

The German girl paid for my rail ticket to Madrid in exchange for
escorting her and two of her friends on the train. It was a dangerous
journey for women to take without a male in those days. Marco Polo had
entered into a pact with Charles P. by that stage. They'd formed an
alliance to keep the Mahjee and Feeble in a secondary position.

Due to the influence of Marco Polo I left my family in the south of Spain as easily as I'd left my blood family. I was unable to form deep, lasting attachments with people while Polo or Puddlejumper had me in their grasp. They wanted none of that. Marco was only interested in the journey; he despised anything that even vaguely resembled a destination.

When we arrived in Madrid the German girl gave me another gift – a bus ticket to London. By the time I arrived back in England the rifts between the splintered parts of myself were widening every day. Marco Polo, the Pilgrim, had become the dominant aspect and he'd sublimated Puddlejumper to the point where the two of them virtually merged into one.

As soon as I arrived in England I went straight to Glastonbury. It was a place I'd visited before; I'd gone there searching for the Holy Grail and made many acquaintances. But that's another story.

I had some vague notion that I'd be healed of my autism if I washed myself in the Holy Well. I wanted to be cleansed so I could begin the delicate task of reinventing myself. I wanted to acknowledge the miracle of surviving the Moroccan adventure. I thought I could cement the lessons I'd learned with some sort of ritual. But before I had a chance to do that, I fell in with a strange group of people; not surprising really when you consider the new age nature of Glastonbury. I took part in trance-dance exercises inspired by the Sufi tradition. In a short while I was surprised to find folks were coming to me for advice about trance and accessing ecstatic states. Then I was surprised to find the dance work-shops were suddenly handed over to me to run.

Meditation and trance were daily practices for me. I no longer considered there was anything remarkable about my ability to enter into other states of consciousness. The mountains, hills, valleys and forests of the Far Country were well known to me. I didn't need drugs to get me there. To me trance was just one point on the long spectrum of shut-down.

I bathed in the Holy Well of Glastonbury every day for a week, but all I got out of it was a chill, a fever and loose bowels. Then I heard about a fellow in Ireland who conducted sweat-house ceremonies in accordance with Native American tradition. I immediately tracked his phone number down and got in touch. I arranged to meet the fellow in Dublin. I was desperate for healing. I abandoned all my other commitments and left on the next bus.

The sweat-house was to be one of the most profound experiences of my life. I believe if I hadn't chanced upon it I might not have been able to move forward with my life or to have faced the coming challenges. It opened my eyes to many truths about myself that I'd been absolutely blind to in the past.

> *Dress a goat in silk and it's still a goat.*
> (Old Irish proverb)

Mother used to call me a goat. I used to identify very strongly with that little saying. I thought it referred to the hopelessness of my situation. Before I learned to accept myself I used to pray every morning and night to God; begging Him to transform me into a human. As I waited outside the sweat-house I drifted off into one of my trances perhaps brought on by intense prayer.

I woke just at the very instant my head pitched forward toward my chest. I snapped my eyes open. I was in the semi-darkness on my knees. I realised I must have dozed off. A few steamy breaths escaped my lips. The late evening air was so crisp and chilly my face tingled. I could hear a slow, steady drum-beat, throbbing just a little faster than the pace of my heart. I wondered if I walked into the Far Country.

Heavy weather had been blowing in off the Atlantic for days, as it often does on the west coast of Ireland in October. The rain had eased to a soft drizzle. Directly behind me there was a burning source of heat and light. I glanced over my shoulder. Seductive flashes of flame beckoned, 'Come closer. Draw in where I can warm you.'

Marco Polo, the Pilgrim and Charles P. Puddlejumper had convinced me to go in search of the sweat-house. They yearned for strange experiences; experiences other folks didn't consider proper or safe. The Mahjee was happy to tag along for the ride if the whole exercise resulted in some kind of spiritual growth. The protests of Chameleon Feeble were drowned out.

My circle of acquaintances has always included weirdos of various shades and shoe-sizes. Like attracts like, and it's common knowledge that I love meeting interesting characters. To cut a long story short, when I got to Dublin I arranged to meet a certain gentleman then in his mid-forties. I referred to him as Guide.

The rumour was he'd lived with Native Americans and learned about sweat-houses. He claimed to have been initiated into the Faerie traditions of Ireland and to have met with some of the denizens of that realm. Marco Polo was fascinated by all that sort of talk.

At the time I knew very little about shamanic practices. I may not have even heard the word shaman before I set off on this trip to Ireland. I waited a few days in Dublin before a meeting could be arranged and I was getting very excited at the prospect of talking to this fellow about whom I'd heard so much. When he finally turned up at the pub to meet me he came straight over and shook my hand. Guide wasted no time informing me he was a Celtic shaman and that I'd come to the right place if I wanted to be healed.

Feeble experienced a fleeting rush of anxiety, mixed with mild disappointment, as he said that. The Mahjee stepped up to reassure him. I knew by then that if Feeble was uncomfortable with something it had to be challenged. Puddlejumper, always my inner sceptic, screamed at me, 'Watch out! You've got a live one here!'

After that dramatic opener Feeble thought about making a quick getaway. Fortunately, Marco was intrigued enough to want to hear what Guide had to say. He'd been described to me as charismatic and striking. My English friends said he had a touch of the fey about him. I had to agree.

His eyes were a light moss-green that drew you in. Naturally, I had to turn away. Contact of this sort with a stranger is simply too much for me to take. I didn't want to admit I was autistic so I told him I was an extremely shy person.

He launched into a few questions about my general health and fitness. Then he moved on to inquire whether I was a regular drinker. A musician? A storyteller? A dancer? An artist? A poet? Did I meditate or engage in spiritual practices? Was I vegetarian? Was it true I could trance-dance with ease?

My replies clearly pleased him. Soon he was telling me all about his wonderful experiences with a native shaman in the jungles of the Amazon. He'd lived there for two years before he was allowed to take the sacred drink that allows men to see spirits. Puddlejumper came to the conclusion this bloke might be a bloody liar but he was a damn fine story-teller.

Then Guide broached a difficult subject. He'd heard rumours that I was a 'bloody madman'. Was it true? Puddlejumper replied that it depended on your definition of mad and who was he to be asking such a question anyway? A Celtic shaman indeed. Did he think I'd descended from the clouds with the last regular batch of freezing precipitation? Guide laughed and slapped me on the back.

That broke the tension between us. Guide explained he didn't care whether I was mad or not. Mad may equate with bad in Western society but it didn't necessarily hold the same meaning in traditional cultures. Mad, in his opinion, was selling your life in slavery to the bank for a little box made out of brick.

That won Puddlejumper over in an instant. Over three rounds of tea we shared pilgrims' tales as if we were a pair of long-lost friends who had a lot to catch up on. I heard so much talk about the Faerie spirits in that conversation it made my head spin. He told me the sweat-house was a place to encourage visions, further the healing process and nurture epiphanies.

Guide said that ancient people considered the sweat-house a sacred rite, a mystical forge where the four elements combine. A place where the base metal of the body may be transformed into gold. Marco told him it sounded interesting, but Puddlejumper added a little laugh at the end of the sentence.

Suddenly Guide stood up and grabbed his oilskin jacket. 'You're in. I'll meet you at the station tomorrow morning. We'll go down to Galway on the train. There's a sweat-house on Sunday. Invitation only.'

He winked as the Mahjee shook his hand.

'You're a strange one,' he confided. 'All that switching between characters must make life bloody difficult.'

He was the first person ever to point out to me that the disparate aspects of myself were jostling for position. Perhaps it was just becoming more obvious by that stage. I felt extremely exposed. Then he was gone, leaving me suffering a mix of anticipation, apprehension and excitement. Sunday didn't come around quick enough. Next thing I remember I was dozing by the bonfire, waiting to be led into a primitive circular stone hut.

For two days I'd stuck to a strict diet of thin vegetable soup and oat-biscuits. I hadn't eaten anything since before sunrise. The previous night I'd stayed up till after dawn singing, talking and getting to know the others in our group.

Feeble was tired, hungry, cold and a little grumpy and he wasn't at all comfortable about being naked under the woollen cloak wrapped close around my body. There were a dozen of us, mostly women. Another time I attended a sweat-house with 30 people, but this one was designed for a mercifully small circle.

A few of the others had been fasting for a week. They each took a mouthful from a deep bowl of broth. This was not offered to me. Guide told me I had no need of it.

I felt a hand at my shoulder and there was Guide's wife. Without a word she nodded toward the circular stone structure. Earlier in the day we'd completely covered it with tarpaulins, blankets and hides. They were held in place by ropes weighted down with heavy stones. The others were silently filing into the house.

A cowhide covered the door. I knelt down before it to say a little prayer, then the hide lifted and I went in. A lantern hung from the sweat-house ceiling. The flame burned low, revealing a smooth stone bench set around the circular wall. Straw and fresh herbs were strewn over the damp earthen floor. One by one we found our places on the bench, pushed our cloaks back behind us and proceeded to offer one another reassuring smiles. The sweat-house was much bigger on the inside than I'd imagined. There was enough room for everyone to sit without coming into physical contact with the person at either side. This was a great relief to Feeble.

In the middle of the chamber a large stone basin was half-buried in the soil. I knew Guide had built the sweat-house quite recently but I couldn't escape the notion it was a very ancient place. I got the strange feeling this ceremony, or one like it, had been celebrated for generations within those walls.

Outside two more drummers joined the first, adding their own subtle touches to the dreamy, soothing rhythm. Then the lantern went out as Guide sternly issued final instructions.

'Listen to your body,' he advised. 'Leave the sweat-house when your body tells you. Listen to your spirit. Stay in the sweat-house until you've reached your limit. Don't listen to your mind. That's how you got tricked into this bloody ordeal in the first place.'

There was laughter all around, then the cowhide was pulled aside and Guide's brother brought in the first rock from the heart of the fire. It was scarlet-red; radiating an intense heat that reflected off the walls and ceiling. Another two fiery rocks came in.

'Welcome to the womb, ancient ones,' Guide intoned, addressing the glowing trio of stones.

'Welcome,' the others echoed.

Sweet fragrant smoke of burning rosemary scented the chamber. Then came the first ear-splitting hiss as Guide ladled water over the hot rocks. A wave of searing steam hit me, clearing my blocked nasal passages as the heated air penetrated deep into my lungs. The chill I'd caught at the Holy Well vanished completely.

Earlier in the day Guide's wife had shown us a round river-stone carved with elegant double spirals. She passed it to the young woman seated to her left and the next part of the sweat-house ritual began.

'I've come here to be cleansed of my bitterness,' the woman confessed. 'I haven't been the same since my boyfriend left me.'

When she was done the stone passed on again to the left. The man next to her revealed that depression had brought him to the sweat-house to seek healing. And so on. Some delivered prayers to Saint Bridget or Christ; a few spoke of feeling frightened. One young man with an angelic voice sang a moving lament, mourning the passing of his mother. It was all about rights of passage, turning points and healing.

By the time I held the speaking stone, sweat was rolling off my body, running over my skin in rivulets. I never knew I had so much water in me. I cradled the stone in my lap, tracing the spirals with a finger.

'I'm not sure why I'm here,' I admitted. 'When I heard about it I just had to come and take part. It feels like some kind of an initiation.'

There were gentle murmurs of recognition around the chamber. I handed the stone on as a cool metal bucket, half-full of water, brushed against my leg. What a welcome surprise that was. My throat was parched. I swallowed two ladles' worth while I listened to the woman on my left calmly talk about being raped as a little girl. When she was done I passed the bucket on to her.

By the time the last participant had his say, I was afraid I was going to pass out from the heat. Then the lantern was turned up and Guide sat opposite with a broad grin on his face.

He was holding the stone up above his head. He reminded me of that bloody preacher I'd dragged off the stage at school. It was all so theatrical. Puddlejumper was just about to say something derisive when the cowhide lifted, ushering in a welcome gust of cool air.

While Guide's brother brought in more rocks the water-bucket did the circuit. During the next round of steaming we all sang songs together. It didn't last as long as the first round. The third round we all broke into a mournful keen. When that round ended half a dozen sweaters left their seats to go outside.

After the sixth round of rocks came in I decided I'd had enough. When I passed under the cowhide it felt like I was emerging from the womb. I poured cold water over my body and stood shivering by the fire with the others.

One of the women who'd taken a mouthful of broth was staring into the fire. She looked as if her spirit had stepped out of her body and left it behind. Guide touched me on the arm and told me to go back in.

The night went on like that into the next day. Eventually I forgot all about the other people I was sharing the lodge with. I must have drifted off into a kind of sleep. It wasn't like any sort of shut-down I'd ever experienced.

Feeble felt so out of place I think he completely retreated into some deep part of me as he'd never done before. Marco Polo and Puddlejumper stayed on for a while before they too retreated into the darkness. The Mahjee was the last to go.

Eventually the image of the burning gum tree came back to me. It was so vividly there in my mind that I had to shield my face from the ferocity of the flames. I watched it burn as I'd done when I was a boy. All the emotions I'd felt at that time washed over me. All the emotions I'd suppressed also hit me and I cried and sobbed for a long while, lamenting the loss of the green tree-man and King Koala.

I cried for Miss and Tantrika and all the people I'd had to leave behind me on my journey. It was as if the walls had finally broken down and I was freed of all the sorrow that had haunted me throughout my life.

For the first time I felt genuine anger at Mother and Father for abandoning me to an institution; even though I'd managed to escape that fate.

I felt a terrible rage that people like Auntie had called me a worthless sinner and put my strangeness down to the work of the Devil. Or told me I deserved punishment for my sins.

I stirred when a cup of cold water was placed at my mouth. Someone checked my pulse and looked under my eyelids. I asked what time it was. It was the Colonel who replied. In perfect English he said it was time to go home. I looked up and he was standing there in his full uniform. He took off his hat and wiped the sweat away from his brow as I'd seen him do so many times before.

I closed my eyes and drifted back into my trance-dream. I felt the Mahjee, Puddlejumper and Marco Polo coalesce into one entity for whom I could not find a name. Feeble was not among them. It was as if he'd melted into nothing and been flushed out of me with my sweat.

A woman's hand touched my shoulder. I looked up again and it was Tantrika. She was naked and smiling broadly at me as she often did. I've never known anyone who smiled as much as she did.

'What are you doing here?' I asked her.

'The question is, what are *you* doing here?' she replied with a laugh.

The next thing I felt something tugging at my shoulder. I glanced behind me and Tantrika disappeared. When I put my hand up to my shoulder I felt cold, scaly fingers with sharp talons that dug painfully into my flesh. I turned my head to see what had hold of me.

It was a dragon's claw and it was drawing blood. I could hear the beast breathing hot and hard at the back of my neck. I wasn't afraid at all. I wasn't upset in the slightest; even though I knew for certain the creature had a firm grip on me and would not be prised away no matter how hard I tried to push him off.

'You're mine,' the dragon hissed. 'All mine.'

I was surprised that I wasn't driven frantic by the presence of this beastie. I realised it had always been there, or at least for so long that I hardly noticed its presence any more.

I smelled eucalyptus oil. I asked the dragon to show me its face so I could know what my enemy looked like. It laughed and told me it was not my enemy. It was my friend. It told me to look in the mirror if I wanted to see it. In the next instant there was a huge polished steel shield before my eyes. The surface shimmered like the water in the stone basin.

When the ripples died away I saw a huge tree-like creature with one tear-filled eye and many leaves shaped exactly like mouths with toothy smiles. I was looking at the self-portrait I'd painted in 12th grade.

'It's time to go home,' the dragon hissed.

The whole chamber echoed with his words. Familiar voices of people I hadn't seen in years repeated the phrase until someone touched me on the shoulder again and put a cup of cold water to my lips.

I looked up and Guide was smiling at me. When he spoke his Irish accent was gone. He sounded English. Then his face transformed into the old man who'd looked after me in the Moroccan village after the *gitanos* had robbed me.

'Go home, fool,' was all he said.

I asked Guide to help me out of the sweat-house. The next thing I knew I was lying on a mattress by the fire. It was night again. Everyone else was wrapped in blankets, seated around the flames. No one spoke for a long while.

I drifted off to sleep as a woman crawled close under the blanket with me. She may have fancied a sexual encounter but I just wanted to sleep. As the sun rose, the rain-clouds cleared and I woke up. Someone handed me a bowl of porridge, swimming in butter, cream and honey.

I downed a couple of litres of water; I was incredibly thirsty. Then I went to crash in the back of a van and I didn't wake up again until just before dusk. It took a few days for me to recover from the physical ordeal of the sweating. After that I felt like a new person, but I'm very glad I was physically fit.

All these years since, I've kept the visions to myself. I've told the story of the sweat-house many times, but I've never before talked about the dragon, the Colonel, Tantrika or the old man. I didn't want people to think I was mad. Nowadays I don't care so much about that sort of thing. Mad doesn't have the exclusively negative connotations it used to. Like so many things it's not black and white for me.

The sweat-house was the first time the shame-dragon spoke to me. Feeble and the others had briefly healed their differences and relinquished their individuality. For a short while I was a whole person. For the first time since I was 12 years old I was able to sleep peacefully.

Over the next few nights many dreams came to me. I dreamed about Mother forcing a rolling pin into my arse. I dreamed about having my eyebrow stitched up by the Colonel with Tantrika as his nurse. Strange stuff; but then that's me.

In one dream I was a raven seated high up in an impossibly tall gum tree that was being buffeted by a summer gale. All around me were hundreds of other cackling ravens, all involved in a furious debate. At the very top of the tree brushing the gathering storm clouds, there was a mighty queen-raven larger than the rest. Though she presided over the rowdy meeting it seemed as if none of the birds were taking any notice of her.

One instant there were hundreds of birds flapping their black feathers and cawing; in the next they'd been drawn into the heart of the tree to become one with it. They just melted into the branches. With startling clarity I knew I was that tree. After a great struggle I managed to lift my branches up to the sky just as a bright spear of lightning struck me at the fingertips and set my oily leaves on fire.

The smell of burning eucalyptus oil was stinging my nostrils. I frantically waved my arms about, but that just made the fire fiercer. I screamed and screamed as the blaze caught in my hair and consumed me. I woke with my arms stretched up to the ceiling and my heart pounding in my chest. The woman who'd crawled close to me by the fire a few nights earlier was straddling my body and she was naked. I didn't know for a while whether or not I was dreaming. I pushed her away and curled up by myself.

Soon after my sweat-house experience I made the decision to travel back to Australia. Even though I was certain I'd end up in hospital, I realised I was gradually becoming stranger and stranger. I glimpsed for the first time that I risked permanently splintering into several component parts.

I began to understand what parts of me each of them represented. The Mahjee was the spiritual seeker disgruntled with material pursuits. He was based on my memories of Auntie's husband – Uncle.

Uncle was an old man. He was often silent and contemplative. Whenever he spoke people listened because his words were usually wise and thoughtful. He knew how to cut to the heart of any matter. He was a simple chicken farmer who dismissed his wife's Christian beliefs out of hand; yet he was a man of the spirit.

As I journeyed on through life the Mahjee took on the attributes of other people I met who were travelling the spiritual path. There were Buddhist monks and Hindu holy men and women among them.

Puddlejumper was the one who loved life and a good laugh. He also retained the propensity for rage that had been a feature of my early life. I know now that his character was closely based on Pop.

It wasn't until after Pop had passed away that I learned what sort of man he'd really been. When the First World War broke out in 1914 he was swept up in the patriotic fervour that gripped Australia. He volunteered for the Australian Light Horse and worked in the army barracks in Brisbane as a farrier-blacksmith.

As soon as he heard his regiment was being sent to reinforce the troops at Gallipoli, Pop had second thoughts about going off to war. His instincts told him he was doomed to die if he stayed with the Light Horse. The cavalry soldiers were being trained as infantry for the trenches. Pop was given a rifle and ordered to take part in exercises with everyone else.

One day before the convoy sailed he left his uniform on the side of a fast-flowing creek and he simply swam away from the war. The army assumed he'd drowned so he was discharged as dead. He changed his name, moved to Darwin and continued working as a blacksmith. When the Light Horse stopped in Darwin months later on their way to the war he shoed their horses. No one recognised him.

What he'd done was almost unthinkable at the time. He would've been shot as a coward and a deserter if they'd ever caught up with him. He always felt ashamed for leaving his friends, and he lived all his life with the expectation that one day he'd be discovered and brought to account. The fact that all the boys he'd enlisted with were killed in the Battle of the Nek probably salted the wound of his guilt.

After the war Pop went wild. He married two women at the same time, had at least three families in different parts of the country and took to the bottle. He lived his life to the full and never let anyone push him around. When the Second World War broke out he went off to work in the essential industry of coal-mining so he wouldn't be called up for military service.

Puddlejumper was a lot like him. Charles P. lived to have a good time and whenever he was running the show he never put himself out for anyone. He believed that life was short and had to be enjoyed no matter what the cost. Rage, anger and shame were Puddlejumper's shared legacies with Pop. He was also the most secretive of all my characters and yet he was also the one who laughed the most. He loved stories though he wasn't a particularly good storyteller.

Marco Polo was, and still is to this day the Pilgrim aspect of me. He lived to learn; he was the one who grasped languages and revelled in new experiences. Of all the characters, I relate to Marco closest of all. Marco was the artist and the musician. Later, he shared the Mahjee's interest in shamanism, spirituality and Tantra. Marco Polo was the aspect of me that could tell a good story.

Puddlejumper loved to listen to him tell his tales. In those times of my life when I was most alone Charles P. would get Marco to recite his stories to keep him entertained. I believe this is how I came to remember some obscure details of my early life even though I forgot many major incidents that happened.

Chameleon Feeble was the frightened one who'd do anything to keep the peace. He started out based on Father. For all his apparent toughness and his frightening manner Father was, and remains, the worst coward I've ever met. He wasn't the kind of coward who'd desert the army in time of war. He was too much of a coward ever to do that sort of thing. He was the kind of coward who supports ideas, prejudices and principles because everyone else does. The kind of coward who might have watched the cattle cars being loaded with Jews in Germany and believed it was the right thing because the government said so.

But worse, far worse than his cowardice and prejudices, Father was also the laziest man I've ever met. He had a propensity for doing nothing that was truly breathtaking. He'd wheedle his way out of anything that had the whiff of work about it. At the same time he was a bully of the worst order. In my experience bullies are little more than lazy cowards. He had me so frightened as a child I'd shit myself when he raised a hand to me. He lied to me about the way the world works and justified his thieving, lying ways by telling me everyone was a crook.

I've often wished Father had been someone worthy of looking up to. It might have changed the course of my life. But he wasn't worth very much at all. He was a selfish, self-centred little man with no conscience, no heart and no ambition other than to stay safe, well-fed and warm.

Over the years Feeble has grown apart from Father. While they may have started out very similar I'm proud to say Chameleon Feeble didn't end up much like Father at all. These days Feeble has become much closer to his counterpart, the Mahjee.

None of my characters liked having rules and strictures imposed upon them. All of them, joined together as one, constituted the real me. But they didn't join together often. They were always involved in some dispute or other. Sometimes I couldn't get any peace from their arguments and fighting.

I knew I needed help. I decided it would probably be best to face my worst fears and hand myself in to the mental hospital at Goodna. I first went back to London, got a job and saved up the airfare as quickly as I could.

Before I returned to Australia I attended another sweat-house in Ireland supervised by Guide. It opened up a lot more for me but I didn't experience the sort of visions and direct messages I got from the first one.

Somehow I managed to keep a lid on the splintering until I arrived in Brisbane. By then I decided I needed to speak with Mother about what had happened to me. I went straight from the airport to the family home. I knocked on the door. My sister answered.

'Oh. It's you,' she said, then she slammed the door again.

I knocked once more. Mother opened it and told me to go away. I said I didn't have anywhere to stay and I wanted to tell her about my journey overseas.

'Have you been overseas?' she asked in surprise. 'I thought you might have gone to Sydney. I didn't think you had it in you to go further.'

It was a brief conversation. Mother didn't want to talk but she offered a place to sleep for the night. Father wouldn't have any of that. He told me to bugger off or he'd call the police.

I left and wandered around for a few hours unsure of what to do. Marco Polo took over for the first time in months. He got me on the main highway. I hitched south to the state border where I found a room in a youth hostel. In a few days I had a job there and I'd forgotten all about handing myself in to Goodna.

Marco Polo loved the hostel. He was bitter at being forced to return to Australia. Queensland at that time was still a sleepy backwater where nothing much happened. The hostel was always full of backpackers from all over the world.

For a while the splintered parts agreed to integrate into one another and work as a team until I could come to some decision about what to do. I gathered a few folks around me who I felt I could trust. Eventually I was promoted to manager and settled in to running the youth hostel.

A year later there were stories in the newspapers about some terrible abuses that had taken place within the mental health system. I read them with dismay because I still intended to hand myself in eventually. However, I began to have second thoughts.

On my travels in Europe I'd met a couple who were actors. They lived in Sydney and they were studying with a small regional theatre company. They visited my hostel one weekend and we all recognised one another immediately. They seemed like such accepting people that I promised I'd visit them if I ever went to Sydney.

After living in London for a long while and travelling the world, Marco Polo began to get restless again. He wasn't satisfied with a small seaside town any more. So I quit my job and I headed south to the big smoke – Sydney – the largest city on the continent.

My instincts must have been firing. I couldn't have gone at a better time. I walked out of the hostel and into the arms of one of the most unexpected life-changing miracles it's ever been my good fortune to experience.

I rolled up at the house of this couple and they welcomed me with open arms. I shared their house for a few months and got a job as assistant to the director of the theatre company. I was so happy that I forgot all about handing myself in to Goodna or seeking help for the splintering.

Sydney satisfied Marco's yearning for adventure, Puddlejumper's desire for a good time and in the bookshops of the city the Mahjee furthered his spiritual studies. Feeble could hide himself away while the others enjoyed themselves.

I met a woman and we became very good friends. It was a friendship like the one I'd had with Miss. Charles P. Puddlejumper fell in love with her. Feeble was infatuated. The Mahjee was grateful to be able to have a partner with whom to share Tantric practices. Marco Polo was the only one who was put out by this relationship. He didn't want to be tied down. He was bitter and suspicious because numerous women had taken sexual advantage of me in the past. Mother's refusal to talk hadn't reassured him about females either. The others may have been opening up to the possibility of accepting love but Polo refused to be vulnerable.

As the director of the theatre got to know me he told me I should consider becoming an actor. I had a fine singing voice by then, I could play a few instruments I'd picked up along the way, and Marco Polo loved telling stories. I took all of these attributes for granted and never thought I could be an actor. Nor did I have a desire to.

Most of the male actors I knew seemed like quite petulant, immature and insecure people. I certainly didn't want to risk ending up like that. I thought I had enough problems to be going on with, thank you very much. I told him I was more than happy remaining an assistant.

But the director didn't let me off that easily. On my behalf, he put in an application to one of the top drama schools in the country. When the confirmation letter arrived from the university I wasn't impressed. I was upset that the director had gone behind my back, but he convinced me to audition. He made the point that it was the only way I'd ever get into university without repeating 12th grade all over again.

I learned a piece by Shakespeare and something modern and I fronted the audition panel. They got me to sing a song. By then I'd been singing for a living on the waterfront in Spain and I'd sung in folk clubs in England and Ireland. The panel sat back stunned as I presented my song. I must be honest – I didn't care whether I got in or not. Perhaps that's why I was so relaxed about the audition.

Out of 500 bright-eyed hopefuls the panel chose 33 to be a part of the course for the next year. I was one of them. I could hardly believe my luck. I hadn't even been trying hard. Of course I had to accept a position. It was the chance of a lifetime.

Suddenly I'd achieved a goal I'd almost forgotten about. I was a university student. Marco Polo was overjoyed to be in a position where he'd be learning new skills every day of the week. Puddlejumper was extremely excited; the potential for fun was greater than he'd ever known.

The Mahjee saw it as an opportunity to explore strategies for emotional healing, and for indulging his love of spiritual exploration. However, he realised his solitude was going to be severely compromised so he forced the others to make a deal. He'd go to university but they'd have to grant him an equal amount of time in solitude later. An alliance was formed.

All three gave Feeble a very hard time. They pressed him to stand behind them and not to come out. If they wanted to pass the course it would require hard work, stamina and commitment. As the weakest link he had the potential to ruin everything for the rest of them.

As it turned out Chameleon Feeble was just as valuable to the equation as the others. He was the one who knew the secret of mimicry, one of the essential skills of an actor. Even though none of them wanted to pursue a career in the theatre, they were still enrolled in a practical degree course in acting.

Marco Polo enrolled me in extra electives besides the ones I was required to take. They included glass-making, ceramics, photography, performance art and a creative writing unit. I was attending a total of almost 60 hours of classes a week with rehearsals on top of that.

The mother of the woman I was in a relationship with warned me I would never be accepted in her family because I wasn't good enough for her daughter. After that, Marco Polo easily convinced the others to abandon the relationship. He justified it by saying that she'd only end up hurt anyway when I was committed to a mental hospital.

Also, I was so exhausted at the end of each week I could barely crawl into bed at night. I was at the very brink of burn-out within the first two months of study. I couldn't be in any sort of relationship. I've often regretted leaving her, but it all turned out well for her. She has the family she craved now. I wouldn't have been a good father to her children.

Feeble protested the rapid changes in my life by refusing to take a back seat any longer. He mourned for years over the loss of that friendship and never forgave Marco Polo for ending it. However, as soon as the word got out that I was single I was being pressured into sexual liaisons with a number of different women in my theatre course.

Feeble was so shell-shocked at the time that I just accepted a lot of situations I felt uncomfortable with. I now know this sort of reaction is quite common among folks suffering post-traumatic shock. I simply did as I was told without questioning the rights and wrongs.

I needed nurturing and I was just waking up to the fact that it was as necessary as fresh air and good food to my survival. Marco Polo permitted the sexual encounters as a kind of trade-off with the Mahjee and Puddlejumper, but he was careful to make sure no woman got past my entrenched defences.

Despite the incredible workload and the extra electives I'd enrolled in I took up painting around this time. I stretched canvasses over bamboo poles that had been lashed together in weird shapes. Then I painted designs I'd seen carved on standing stones in Ireland, Britain and Europe – spirals, circles, dots and zigzags.

This wasn't my first crack at being a painter. On my pilgrimage I'd taken up stretching canvasses over weirdly shaped sticks. I ended up holding two exhibitions of my work in Germany and selling out all my paintings. My newer concoctions were much the same, except that I was adding these strange Stone Age designs.

One of my lecturers visited my house one evening to drop off a book. He was speechless when he saw every spare inch of wall-space taken up with my bizarre sculptural forms. He arranged for me to exhibit my artworks in the foyer of the theatre during performances. The first exhibition sold out in days.

I compulsively went on painting and stretching canvasses. I continued selling these weird constructions as fast as I could make them. In a few months I had a waiting list of collectors wanting my work. I used to turn buyers away if I didn't feel completely comfortable with them.

I should have spent the money I earned from painting on food but I was collecting books. Not text books for study. I was reading about the various religious and spiritual traditions of the world. The Mahjee had introduced me to this obsession but I had taken it up with enthusiasm. I read about Islam, Zoroastrianism, Zen, Native American traditions and ancient Celtic beliefs.

The other thing that I spent my money on was a hand-made Celtic harp. Ever since the days of my pilgrimage I'd been fascinated by the small brass-strung harp. I'd heard a performance by a famous Breton harper, Alan Stivell, and promised myself I'd learn the instrument one day.

The harp took a year for the builder to deliver. In that time I watched every video I could find of traditional Irish, Scots and Breton harpers performing. I would have listened to harp music all day long if time and other commitments had permitted. By the time I had it at home I knew everything there was to know about harps of this type.

I set aside three hours a day to practise but I rarely played less than four. Within six weeks I was performing as if I'd been doing it all my life. In 12 weeks I was composing new pieces for the harp. In a few more months I was confident enough to perform on stage and started earning a modest living playing for weddings and the occasional concert. Twelve months after I took delivery of the harp it had already paid for itself.

I didn't think much about playing the harp. I certainly never questioned whether I could do it. I didn't consider my paintings were very special either until someone asked me why I was wasting my time at university. Without setting out to become an artist I was suddenly a very successful one. I suppose my seemingly effortless accomplishments helped fuel the rising jealousy of my peers.

I suffered a rage attack at university during rehearsals for final assessments but I'm glad I did. I was working with one of my classmates on a two-hander scene depicting the conflict between two brothers. He refused to learn his lines or rehearse. As the date of the assessment approached he told me he'd decided to drop out and he was only going through with the assessment to help me out. Unfortunately he wasn't much help. On the morning of the assessment he turned up and we ran through the lines until I was confident he knew the part. The moment we stepped out on stage I found out why he'd decided to drop out. He had stage fright. He mumbled through his opening speech and I started fuming. All of a sudden I heard my cue line and I exploded with rage. Somehow I managed to stick precisely to the script but I let him know in no uncertain terms that I was really pissed off with him. Poor bugger. He nearly wet himself with fright. I have a very powerful voice and I know how to use it. From my point of view the scene went terribly and I expected to fail the assessment.

The surprise came a week later when my acting tutor called me in to his office. It seems no one even noticed how enraged I'd become. It suited the character and the piece perfectly. I got a high distinction.

By the end of first year Marco Polo had managed to alienate most of the other students in my class. He'd made no secret of the fact that I didn't want to be an actor. I just wanted to get myself an education and learn as much as I could.

I didn't understand that most of them had been waiting all their lives for this opportunity. It was a fairy-tale dream-come-true for them. They simply couldn't understand my attitude. It smacked of arrogance. A petition went the rounds demanding that I be stood down from the course and my place given to someone who was devoted to the craft of acting. Actors can be such pretentious nobs.

I was informed about the petition by the dean of the faculty but I was also assured no action would be taken. I didn't realise at the time that I was one of the most promising actors in my class. This was because I was working so hard I didn't have much time to be distracted by socialising with my peers or worrying about whether I had what it takes to be a success.

My optimism always tends to see me through. I don't know where it comes from. I just don't believe there's much point in worrying about things that might never happen. Life's hard enough. Why make it harder by fretting?

The other thing was I'd got to the point where I didn't make too much of anything anyone told me about myself any more. I'd learned to take attacks on my character with a grain of salt. As for praise; well, I really didn't have much experience of it, so I ignored that too. I still don't take much notice of praise.

The women I dallied with never ever spoke about me to me. They were more interested in other topics of conversation, when there was much conversation. Marco Polo preferred intellectual and spiritual isolation; the Mahjee rigorously enforced it.

At the beginning of second year I had to drop all my elective subjects because I hadn't been eating properly and I was becoming sick, suffering from malnutrition and exhaustion. I still attended photography class when I had the chance because I was involved with an art student in a project and I didn't want to let her down.

By then it was becoming apparent to those who worked with me that I wasn't quite the same as everyone else. I was a dark horse and I must have seemed very strange. I managed to live on a government student benefit supplemented by sales of paintings and a few gigs as a musician here and there. Most of my colleagues had wealthy families who supported them. They didn't need to work and they were always well fed.

I determined I wasn't going to let exhaustion slow me down too much. I learned to play the bass saxophone in three days for one production. In fact I could pick up any instrument and play it well without too much practice. I took music for granted.

I always had all my lines learned perfectly before the first rehearsal. All the characters I was given to play were also fully developed when I attended the first rehearsal. I liked to do that so the character would have the opportunity to grow during the rehearsal process. If I hadn't done that I would've died of boredom.

My singing improved further and I was also blessed with a deep, rich speaking voice that didn't require as much daily exercise as my peers. I had more life experience than anyone I knew, though I didn't understand that at the time. I adapted very quickly to new situations.

The thing I loved most was working with masks. The Mahjee soon took up mask productions with enthusiasm. I could see that a marriage of mask performance and spirituality was a very powerful tool for accessing other states of being and consciousness. Masks were also potent symbols for my shattered state of existence; though I didn't understand that at the time. I only know I sensed I might later be able to heal myself through a familiarity with masks.

When the university began a cultural exchange programme with the tribal elders of Pitjantjatjara-land in Central Australia the Mahjee was the first to put his hand up. Marco Polo and the Mahjee moved closer together during this period when they were learning about the Dreamtime and the awe-inspiring spirituality of the Pitjantjatjara people.

I was fascinated with their traditions. One custom in particular caught my imagination. When someone passes away the Pitjantjatjara never mention their name again. If they have to talk about the deceased person they'll say; 'that fella' or 'his sister'. They believe using the name of the dead calls up their spirit and disturbs their new life in the Dreamtime. It's a tradition that resonated with someone like me who never liked names to begin with.

Since the day I ran away as a five-year-old I'd never been able to get the image of that blackfella in the mango tree out of my head. Whenever he appeared in my dreams he'd be sitting up there feasting on the succulent fruit with the sweet juice running down his chin on to his tattered old suit-coat. It was the memory of him that summoned me to the desert of Central Australia to listen to stories from the people who'd lived on this big island for 40,000 years.

Some of the other students noticed I was also full of contradictions. Everyone knew I'd done poorly at school yet I spoke fluent German, Gaelic and Spanish. I also understood French and had a smattering of Thai and Arabic that had stuck from my great pilgrimage. I was cast in lead roles in most productions and my grades were very good. But my fellow students were always looking for excuses to have me kicked out or reprimanded. The rumour mill was cranked up and it started grinding out prejudice.

There was a small Christian faction in my year – three students who were hoping to get the skills to start an evangelical theatre group. I saw them as trouble-makers who were always questioning the ethics of this or that and wasting everyone's time. They loudly condemned anyone who failed to offer them support and they were always preaching. The worst thing about them was their double-standards. They'd be spouting about the Ten Commandments one day and clumsily breaking rules the next to show how street-wise they were. I viewed them as a troop of spiritual Keystone Cops.

Despite their apparent pettiness, I remained open-minded and accepting of them. When no one else would work with these clowns on an assignment I volunteered. One afternoon they all came around to my house to rehearse and everything seemed to be going well until we had a break for tea.

My bookshelf was inspected. I was reading the Qur'an at that time. I also had a complete set of the Hindu Vedas I was working my way through. I had books on ancient paganism, the Cathars and a copy of the Nag Hammadi manuscripts. Most of the stuff was beyond them. It was a history of witchcraft that caught the attention of the one male in the group. He thumbed through it hissing as he went. Right next to it there was a portfolio of female nudes my photographer friend had taken during her assessments. He soon had his grubby paws on that and I thought the book on witchcraft had been forgotten.

Within a week I heard the old familiar cry of demon. I was accused of being a devil-worshipper and a witch. Witchcraft was cited as an explanation for my uncanny abilities. I laughed when I heard the rumour. I couldn't believe they were serious.

One of the Christian women offered to heal me of my affliction; in private of course. I rejected her kind offer. I'd heard it all before so I didn't take too much notice. In fact all the furore achieved was to attract folks into my circle who had a slightly more Gothic fashion sense. Marco Polo expected trouble, but then again he always expects trouble. Much to my annoyance he's usually right of course.

Toward the end of second year I was accused of being a psychopath by one of the more jealous, insecure males in my class. I've never found out the basis for this accusation though I'm sure my behaviour was strange enough to warrant some suspicion and perhaps concern. I guess I looked like I might be schizophrenic.

I was under enormous pressure to conform and that has always caused me problems. I had one rage attack in the privacy of my own home after class one day. It was so powerful I realised I couldn't go on keeping it all bottled up. I went to see a student counsellor who told me I should think about taking a year off. I wasn't about to consider that option. I was having the time of my life. Every aspect of me was enjoying theatre school. But as the weeks went on I found fewer and fewer of my classmates were willing to have anything to do with me. I was being treated the same way as the Christians.

I kept getting very good grades and performing well under pressure. I always have. But I'd never been that exhausted before and the splintered parts of me tend to move further apart when I'm under attack. Marco Polo panicked thinking he might have reached the end of the line. I withdrew even further behind a wall of secrecy.

Eventually all the prejudiced hostility I'd stirred up came to a head. The performance pieces for graduation year were posted and it was widely rumoured I would be cast in the male lead for one of the plays because the character would have suited me perfectly. A few days after the list was posted I received a visit from three of my classmates at my home.

I'd hardly opened the door when I knew something bad was going to happen. The boys didn't waste time with pleasantries. They got straight down to business. Two of them held me down while the other one beat the living crap out of me. When he got tired the other two stepped in and had a go. They knew what they were doing; they'd all been to boarding schools. I guess I should be grateful they didn't bugger me senseless before I blacked out. I was so badly knocked about I had to take three days off class. Feeble was well and truly petrified. He's never been able to abide violence. He's never been able to understand it.

Marco Polo and the Mahjee were deeply shocked but they agreed that Feeble wouldn't be able to take another vicious invasion like that. After the beating I lapsed into a catatonic haze for about 24 hours. The other characters suddenly became very protective of Feeble.

Marco Polo went to the dean of the faculty and told him what had happened. Then he formally deferred my studies for one year so I would not have to deal with those cowardly bullies again.

It was the best move I ever made. With the kind help of sympathetic lecturers I got a job as an artist-in-residence at a community arts facility. I exhibited new paintings and worked at odd jobs, and my health improved over the course of the year off.

I had the opportunity to speak with Mother during this break in my studies. I don't know why she decided to talk to me but I'm grateful that she did. By then I had many questions to ask her about myself and I was even considering going to Goodna to seek treatment.

Mother had changed. She'd lost her edge. She told me my name had been taken off the waiting list for Goodna when I was 18 because I was considered an adult by that time. She'd lied to me about signing the papers in the hope that she'd be rid of me once and for all. She never apologised for what she'd done. In her opinion she'd been doing the best for her family. I was a mental case and I would never have amounted to anything. She didn't want me hanging around cluttering up her life and continuing to be a financial burden.

Father had decided I was useless and hadn't spoken about me since I'd left home. I visited her twice in Brisbane without the knowledge of Father. He wouldn't have allowed it. She told me her story, much of which I'd never heard before. Mother also revealed much about my early life that surprised me. She told me she'd never forgive me for turning out the way I did and that I should thank my lucky stars she'd agreed to see me. As far as she was concerned I was still a retard and I belonged in hospital. She said my extended family never forgave me for being (as she and they thought) a homosexual. Every one of them had expressed to her the hope that they'd never see me again.

Mother hoped I was still ashamed of myself for hurting so many people who would have preferred to care for me. She never understood that it wasn't my decision to be the way I am. She never accepted me. Father had launched into an affair with a younger woman after I'd left home. Mother blamed his infidelity on me and so did the rest of the family. I'd caused more trouble than I was worth, she told me.

Despite her bitter hatred the Mahjee felt immense compassion for Mother. Charles P. Puddlejumper thought she was pathetic. Marco Polo was angry. Chameleon Feeble just wanted her to hug him close and tell him everything would be all right. It was one of those occasions when his wish wasn't granted.

I stayed in contact with Mother over the next year but it was difficult. I had to call her when Father and my sister were out. They certainly wouldn't have tolerated me talking with her.

When I returned to university I was given the male lead in a graduation performance that was to tour the United States. It was the first time the university had sent a touring company anywhere. I couldn't believe my luck. It was worth a beating from my classmates.

I had such a wonderful time in America. Marco Polo was the star of the show and he was treated like a king. I still encountered awful prejudice from my classmates, but the males in my new year were wimps. They couldn't have put a spine together amongst the lot of them. And Puddlejumper wouldn't have let any of them get away with intimidating me anyway.

At the end of the year a theatrical agent approached me but I declined his offer. I'd had enough of theatre. I just wanted a rest. A career in theatre just wasn't to be.

I rang Mother for one of our prearranged chats and my sister answered the phone. I asked to speak with Mother. She replied I'd better call the hospital. She wouldn't tell me what was going on.

'This is all your fault,' she snapped, and hung up.

I telephoned every hospital in Brisbane until I tracked Mother down. She'd been diagnosed with terminal cancer six weeks earlier. She hadn't told me because she didn't want me turning up and causing a scene with Father. The cancer was extremely aggressive and had spread to her whole body from a melanoma on her face. I borrowed the money for a flight to Brisbane. I went to the hospital, but Father had not listed me as family and I had to fight to be allowed to see her even briefly.

By then her spirit was already wandering in a deep, drug-induced coma from which she never awoke. When Father heard I was with her he hit the roof. He drove over to the hospital to have me kicked out. She died a few days later without ever saying farewell or making peace with me.

I saw her corpse laid out on the bed. I touched her cold hand. I'm glad I did. Confirmation that she had left this world gave me a great deal of peace. A lot of fear disappeared once I knew she couldn't touch me again. My nightmares were never as bad or as frequent again.

As I stood looking at her lifeless body Father told me I didn't deserve a mother like her. He told me I'd killed her by being such a little bastard. He went on and on like that until a nurse asked me to leave the room because my presence was upsetting Father.

For all the awful words and violence that passed between Mother and me, I was devastated that I hadn't had the opportunity to say good-bye and tell her I'd forgiven her. I'm sure we could have one day become friends if she'd lived. At the funeral I sat next to Nanna, who was then in her nineties. She told me a few more things I didn't know about my child-hood.

Father made it clear that there was nothing for me to inherit. Mother had left everything to her real family. On the steps of the crematorium he told me to bugger off and never come back. Other members of the extended family were polite to me that day but it was clear they shared his opinion. Two of Mother's close friends told me I shouldn't have come to the funeral. I was a bastard and no one wanted to see me. Mother had died because of me, because I had been such a bastard. I heard that over and over again.

I went back to the family home to retrieve my photos and books. Father had already burned them all. I have no photos of myself as a child, as a teenager or in my cadet uniform. He told me he didn't want shit like that cluttering up his house.

Before he told me to bugger off one more time he coldly informed me I wasn't even his son. He reckoned I'd been born out of an affair. He claimed Mother had been involved with some Christian preacher. He reckoned God had punished her for her sins by bringing me into the world. I never believed a word of it.

A cousin drove me to the airport. He didn't speak a word to me the whole way. As soon as I got out of the car he drove off without any word of farewell. I flew to Sydney, caught a train home and walked from the station without remembering any of it. I'd already lapsed into a zombie state from the overwhelming grief and guilt.

Seven hours after I left Brisbane I was seated on my bed at home. I stayed there for two days repeating the words, 'I'm sorry,' over and over again until I'd reached a hundred thousand sorrys. Then I went on to a million and ten million.

To this day I have not been able to forgive myself for her death. I still believe that if I had not been the way I was she could have had a long and happy life. I destroyed her dreams of a happy, loving son and I will never be easy with that.

I tried to contact my sister but she made it clear she didn't want to speak with me. I'd killed her mother. She told me to go away and never come back. A year after Mother died Father told me my sister had married a Texan missionary and gone to live in America. I wondered if he was one of the Fishers of Men. I was instructed never to contact her.

Father warned me that if I ever made contact with him again he'd go to the police and make a formal complaint. He told me he'd written his will specifically to ensure I could never claim any part of his estate. The last thing he ever said to me was, 'If you were a dog we would've shot you.'

No one in my extended family has ever forgiven me for Mother's death. It was made clear to me that I would never be acknowledged or accepted by any of them. Most of them are devout Christians.

After Mother passed over I did not shed a tear because I knew that if I did the flood would not have stopped. Marco Polo took control of my life once again. He guided me through the next few months when sorrow clouded everything. I didn't attend my graduation because I knew I'd be there alone and I couldn't afford the academic robes.

I didn't want to work in the theatre but I needed to pay the rent and I was, by that stage, very ill from creeping malnutrition. My kidneys had been bleeding and I was in a terrible state. But after a few months with a well-paid acting role at a tourist venue I'd begun to recover. Then out of the blue I was offered a teaching position at a junior high school. I snapped it up even though I didn't know the first thing about being a teacher.

It was a fresh start. My gift for optimism kicked in and the Mahjee took over arranging the details. I cut my ties with everyone I knew and turned over a new page of my life. In fact, what I did was to push all the sorrow, guilt, shame and anger down deep into me where I couldn't see it any more because I didn't believe I had the right to feel those things.

To begin with, teaching art and drama in a Catholic junior high school was a wonderful new world of fun and challenges. I was popular with the students and I loved my work. The nuns who ran the school seemed to like my style and for the first time I began to imagine what it would be like to have a normal life like everybody else.

The trouble was, and always has been, that I'm not normal. I'm a freak. I'm a little bastard. I'd managed to land the job because the Mahjee, Charles P. Puddlejumper and Marco Polo had learned a lot in theatre school about maintaining a steady character throughout the performance. Chameleon Feeble was the expert on protocol and he was assigned to hold up the mask the others had constructed.

Everything about me was a mask – a delicate mask made of tissue paper that was barely holding back a seething flood of grief, guilt and shame. It was inevitable that I'd strike trouble. I was, after all, surrounded by devout Catholics. And if there's any group of people in our society who know how to nurture those three dark indulgences, it's Catholics.

Seven

Here's my theory about how the splits within me evolved into characters. I'm made up of three distinct parts. Body, Mind and Spirit. Each one is dependent on the other two and if any one is separated from the others the result is death. I'll give you a run down on each one of them from my point of view.

Body. This is the machine or the vehicle which contains the various aspects of me. The body contains receivers for the senses that give me information about the world through sight, smell, taste, touch and hearing.

When there's a problem with the body, if it's damaged or malfunctions in some way, an alarm goes off. This signal is called pain. Pain isn't real to me. It's just a warning signal that can be turned off or ignored as the occasion requires.

Digestion, breathing and immune system are functions that more or less take care of themselves. Each has a unique system of warnings or indicators that keep these operations going in the background. Hunger, thirst and defecation give signals that must be answered or the body will suffer. Sexual urges and physical addictions give signals out but I recognise that they don't always have to be answered urgently, if at all. When the vehicle wears out or is too damaged to continue, the body dies and returns to the earth.

Charles P. Puddlejumper is the part of me most connected with the body. He loves sensuality, intimacy, dancing, food, shitting, laughing, singing, sex, pain-relief, sleeping and a glass of wine now and then. He enjoys a bit of danger every once in a while as well.

Mind. I consider the mind to be the operating system for my body. In the same way a modern jet aircraft uses computer software to navigate its course or run fuel and flight systems, my mind monitors the various functions of the body.

It also has the capability for learning new tasks that are programmed into it. My hands play the harp, but it's my mind that tells them which strings to touch. My mouth forms the words in German, but my mind instructs it what shapes to make to correct the accent.

Mind also has the ability to reason and to plan for the future based on experience, fears, desires and beliefs. Mind navigates me through the world, finding food and shelter. It clothes the body appropriately and assesses threats. It also has the gift of humour and artistic expression, and above all it has language.

The mind may have several languages stored away in the memory which it can call on. At one stage there were four I was fluent in. Other forms of language are also stored in my mind, such as skills I've learned. The language of paint is one of my favourites. Music is the universal language everyone understands. Sensuality is another common language.

If the mind malfunctions, the body will probably suffer and eventually die. When the body passes back to the earth the mind is also extinguished. I used to confuse myself with mind because it's always on alert and seems to have a voice of its own. I don't see things that way any more.

Marco Polo is the aspect of me who is most connected to mind. He learns languages easily, seeks adventure for the sake of learning new skills and knowledge and enjoys a good debate. He also comes up with clever witticisms to make Puddlejumper laugh. The two of them get on great when it comes to music for singing and dancing or recipes for new exotic dishes. Marco is also the storyteller, the entertainer and the philosopher who's always doing his best to make sense of the world.

★ ★ ★

Spirit. In my view the spirit can be likened to the pilot of the body-vehicle. The spirit is the voyager within, who steps out of the vehicle after the ride is ended and may enter another to take part in another voyage at another time. Spirit is beyond death. When mind and body are extinguished my immortal spirit will move on.

The whole purpose of life is for my spirit to learn and experience as much as possible. I believe I've been incarnated for that purpose alone. Learning and experiencing are at the heart of my spirit.

The Mahjee is that aspect of me most involved with matters of the spirit. He is the one who loves meditation, sweat-houses and any practice that accentuates the experience of being embodied in the vehicle of the body. He is the least pushy of the three aspects yet he's also the one who drives the agenda of my life.

The Mahjee has a flip side – an alter ego, if you like. His other side is Chameleon Feeble and the Mahjee developed from the experience of abuse. I'm lucky Feeble is as weak and wishy-washy as he is. If he had dominated the Mahjee, I think my life may have turned out quite differently.

> *In my garden there are always roses*
> *And sweet scented flowers of every kind.*
> *My garden offers up spinach and herbs,*
> *Onions and garlic, basil and sage.*
> *And tasty culinary delights.*
> *Birds beg for bread.*
> *The soil is moist and dark.*
> *But I wouldn't be much of a gardener*
> *If I didn't get down on my knees, bend my back*
> *And pull up the weeds every once in a while.*

My first months as a teacher went very well. I had terrible trouble with the paperwork because I couldn't trick myself into being interested in it. One of my colleagues offered to help me. She was the head of the art department; a woman who appeared very open-minded and progressive, considering she was also a committed Catholic who believed the AIDS epidemic was God's punishment for homosexuals and Africans. She never explained what the inhabitants of Africa had done to inspire God to wipe them out with a plague, but she sincerely believed they'd done something wrong.

A conservative point of view has never been enough to put me off being friendly with anyone. As the year went on we became quite good friends.

I called my new friend, Cheese. This was because she insisted on referring to the art medium of collage as, wait for it, fromage. I thought this was a hilariously funny bit of word-play until I discovered she really didn't know that fromage was the French word for cheese. When I pointed it out to her she shrugged off my objections saying I didn't know what I was talking about. She'd been an art teacher for ten years. She knew best. Cheese went on making a complete fool of herself every time she used the word in the wrong context. I've never understood that kind of stubbornness.

Despite her narrow-minded social views I liked her because she was patient with me and genuinely seemed to have my best interests at heart. At the time, I was sharing a house with a woman I'd been acquainted with since university days, one of the few people I'd stayed in contact with from those times. One morning, without warning, Cheese questioned my relationship with my housemate. I told her we'd been lovers years earlier but that we'd ended that aspect of our friendship. I prefer to be honest even if it compromises me. I was very naïve about relationships and especially about what someone like Cheese considered acceptable. In time she concluded I wasn't sleeping with my housemate and then she stepped up her pursuit of me.

I was fresh-faced and enthusiastic in those days. I suppose I looked like I was fairly stupid. Thankfully, age has granted me a few wrinkles that make me look less gullible. Chameleon Feeble tended to be the one who dealt with Cheese because she was so intimidating.

I was on shaky ground with all these Christians. I could never tell what the rules were with them. Every Christian you meet has a different interpretation of God's word, a totally different view of morality and they all think they're right.

Cheese convinced me to move into her family house with her and before I knew what was happening we were engaged to be married.

There was no romance involved. I didn't ask her to wed me. One day she simply informed me that's what would be happening. I was taken to meet her parents in the country and then interviewed by her parish priest. Mother was so disconnected from me that she'd never bothered to have me baptised. She didn't think I was worth all the effort. So the priest insisted it should be done as quickly as possible. He also wanted me confirmed before any wedding could take place. I went along with all this because Chameleon Feeble was frightened of being punished for doing the wrong thing.

The Mahjee went to sleep during this period. I don't know what happened to him – he simply disappeared. I was still meditating a minimum of an hour every day. The only time I ever sensed his presence deep in the well of my being was during meditation.

Charles P. Puddlejumper came out whenever I was teaching because the students could relate to him. Marco Polo was always propping Feeble up by drawing on life experience, knowledge and his immense capacity for learning new skills. During this period the transitions between my characters became incredibly smooth, so smooth that the gulfs between them rarely showed.

Once the wedding date was set, Cheese began to be more open with me about herself. She revealed that she was sexually attracted to women more than men. She told me our marriage would have to be open so she could engage in other relationships. I had no objection to that. To be honest I didn't care. In those days I just thought I should do what I was told.

Chameleon Feeble wanted to make Cheese happy. After all, the most satisfying relationships of my life had been built on that very principle. One day I suddenly woke up to the fact that Cheese was very much like Miss. Indeed all her students simply called her Miss. Sadly, in most ways, she wasn't half the woman Miss had been. Cheese espoused ideals of compassion, but she was narrow-minded and selfish. She was deeply suspicious of my daily meditation routine and the philosophical knowledge Marco Polo had acquired over the years.

My personal experience of sexuality through Tantric practices probably frightened her because she simply didn't understand that making love is quite a different experience from sex. At that time I wasn't aware that most people don't know much about love-making. Cheese ridiculed the hour I spent at meditation each day. When that didn't stop me, she began deliberately interrupting it.

As evidence mounted that Cheese wasn't all she seemed, Feeble began to doubt her sincerity. Marco Polo was looking for ways out of my commitment to her. He found his out-option one day when he realised she'd been lying to me over an important matter to do with work. She'd cooked the books, as the saying goes. I realised our marriage would be nothing more than a sham constructed so she could further her career as an administrator. I saw Cheese as a master manipulator.

Before school ended for the year, one of her former students told me he'd been involved in a sexual relationship with her for years. He was very angry at me for stealing her away. The parallels between Cheese and my Miss were astounding.

During the long summer holiday over Christmas the day finally arrived for me to be baptised a Catholic. I went with my fiancée to see the bishop. All the way Cheese was telling me how important it was for a Catholic to renounce Satan. I accepted the baptism and the bishop drove the Devil out of me with the traditional words. Afterwards he privately cautioned me that meditation was a heathen practice unsuitable for the followers of Christ.

On the way home Cheese insisted it was time I stopped meditating altogether. The bishop had instructed me to give up and as a good Catholic I was compelled to obey him. She didn't want the nuns to find out I was into anything that contravened Catholic doctrine. It might damage her career. I reluctantly agreed to cut back my meditation.

Then Cheese insisted I should burn my copy of the Qur'an and the Hindu holy books as well. I laughed at her. I couldn't see what harm they could do. She announced that her family had already disposed of them. She didn't want them in the house. Marco Polo was so shocked he couldn't believe he'd been betrayed by her. Throughout the hungry years of university those books had kept me sane. She told me a good Catholic who'd renounced Satan had no use for pagan ideas and false prophets. Chameleon Feeble tried to stay calm but even he was outraged. It was Mother all over again.

'What right do you have to destroy my books?' I asked her.

'I'm your wife,' Cheese replied. 'I have every right.'

'We're not married yet,' I shot back.

Feeble and Polo were locked in an internal conflict before we'd arrived home. Marco Polo was angry and he could barely hold it all in. The split with Feeble was widening. I don't recall what happened that afternoon except that Marco got some of his books back and took them for safe keeping to his former housemate.

Cheese exploded with jealousy that I'd dared to maintain a friendship with any female, let alone this one in particular. She warned me that being married meant I wasn't permitted to have any other women in my life. I noted that the same rule didn't apply to her.

Marco Polo told me it was time to leave. I packed my things and I walked out. Cheese must have panicked. She must have been concerned I'd speak about her lesbian leanings. It certainly would have put an end to her ambition of becoming a school principal in the Catholic school system. But I'm not the kind to expose anyone to that kind of scrutiny. The next thing I knew the nun in charge of the school rang me to say I was required to undergo a psychological assessment if I was to return to school as a teacher. Cheese had made some accusations about me. I was never told what those accusations were. As a lowly teacher I didn't have the right to know.

I had no choice but to agree to be tested. I went along to see a psychologist. I was open about the abuse I'd suffered as a child but I was careful never to mention autism. I wasn't willing to give up my wonderful life as a teacher and be locked up because of some misguided fanatic. The psychologist diagnosed me with post-traumatic stress disorder. She passed me as fit to teach because I'd developed strategies to overcome the debilitating effects of trauma.

The nuns demanded I attend counselling. I went along to a few counselling sessions after which time the psychologist told me I was fine. I'd learned how to cover my splits, my trauma and my grief to the point where I could bluff my way past any half-hearted counsellor. And believe me, this particular psychologist wasn't as interested in me as my money.

In the two weeks before school commenced everything crashed down around me. The guilt I suffered for the death of Mother and the fear of exposure as a freak led me into one of the most profound catatonic episodes of my life. I'd had breakdowns before, but this one was a tsunami compared to the little waves I'd managed to surf in the past. I cried for a week, seated on my bed in the same spot where I'd begged forgiveness from Mother after her passing. My housemate looked in on me now and then but I had no one to offer me support. The counsellor refused to see me because of a demanding schedule. I couldn't find anyone professional who'd talk to me at short notice.

The Mahjee returned from seclusion to stand by my shoulder and whisper words of encouragement. Marco Polo was so angry he was of no use whatsoever. I think it was the first time I've ever felt such terrible earth-shattering rage at the injustices I'd suffered. Cheese was a minor target of this anger. Father became the focus. His accusations against me; his false claim that I was illegitimate; the way he'd arranged it so I wouldn't be able to say farewell to Mother; all came back to haunt me.

Would no one stand by me? I asked myself this question over and over again. Will no one lend me a helping hand? As if in reply my housemate went away on an extended holiday. She said she wanted to give me the space to calm down.

Charles P. Puddlejumper came up with the idea of self-destruction. I'd never thought about suicide before. It had simply never been an option for me. But I realised I would probably never be accepted for who I was. My family had rejected me. I had no one to turn to.

Before I could follow up on Puddlejumper's suggestion the Mahjee took me along to a psychiatrist, the only professional who had the time to speak with me. He rushed through the consultation in five minutes, prescribed some lithium tablets and told me to come back in a fortnight if my depression hadn't cleared up. I told him I wasn't suffering from a rash, I was feeling suicidal. He shrugged his shoulders and told me I should probably talk to someone about it. I replied that I'd come to him for that reason. As he guided me out the door he explained that I was suffering from a chemical imbalance in my brain.

'Take the pills,' he insisted. 'In a few days your brain chemistry will balance itself out again and you'll be fine. Perhaps you should go out with a few friends and get drunk.' Then he handed me an account for $250. 'Please settle this by the end of the month,' he added as he snapped his fingers cheerily. 'Next please!'

And that sums up my brief flirtation with psychiatry. I took one of the pills but it made me so sick I was throwing up for three days. I flushed the rest down the toilet and returned to my old friend – meditation.

I spent long hours sitting with the anger, hurt and guilt until they'd burned themselves down to a low flame. When it was time to teach again I'd managed to pull myself together enough to go to work, but I was numb.

My colleagues ignored me. A few warned me I wasn't welcome at a good Catholic school. Parents withdrew their children from my classes. I was ostracised. I didn't care. I was given more responsibility in the hope the pressure would force me to leave. I worked longer hours for the same pay. I'm glad the nuns did that to me. The extra workload gave me something to focus on other than my pain. Every day I had to pass my former fiancée in the corridor. Catholic school became a living Hell. My car was regularly vandalised.

One morning I arrived at work to find that my school room had been turned upside down. There was paint everywhere. Thousands of dollars' worth of art materials had been wasted in the destruction. The deputy principal called the police, but before they could arrive Cheese had got some of her students to clean it up. Things like that went on until halfway through the year.

Cheese was finally promoted to deputy principal of a school way out in the bush. I breathed a sigh of relief. But the situation didn't improve. The rumour went around that I was homosexual. The nun in charge called me to her office to explain. Parents were demanding my dismissal. Some colleague from university days with unresolved jealousy issues had come forward to accuse me of being a Satanist, a drug addict and a sodomist; all ridiculous accusations. One night I received a series of death threats over the telephone in the early hours of the morning. The next day I awoke to find the words 'poofter' and 'psycho' painted on my front fence.

Marco Polo and the others held a meeting and with a heavy heart I decided I would have to retire from teaching. Next day I handed in my resignation and almost immediately the intimidation, taunts and attacks on my personal property ceased.

The last three months of school were fairly easy for me. To take my mind off things I started designing intricate Celtic patterns to be printed on t-shirts. I opened a market stall in Sydney and by the end of the year I was making a decent living from my designs. I took up painting again and sold enough to equal my wage as a teacher. I wasn't so nervous about losing my steady income as I had been.

I was so relaxed that the last day of classes took me completely by surprise. The whole school was assembled on the parade ground. The departing teachers were farewelled one at a time. When my name was mentioned every child in the whole place loudly booed and hissed. Most of the teachers joined in. The nuns stood stony-faced and said nothing. I was forced to retreat from the assembly in shame. The deputy principal, a lay teacher, allowed them all to continue like that until I'd gone inside.

He later told me the teaching staff had arranged that special farewell for me. 'Let that be a lesson to you,' he snapped. 'Now get out of my school and don't ever come back.' That was enough to put me off the Catholic church and Christians for life. In my understanding, Christ taught acceptance. I don't recall the part of the Gospel where he endorsed vilification based on vicious gossip. And bishops wonder why people are leaving the church in droves.

I was in shock from my treatment at the school, so I threw myself into my Celtic designs. Creativity is my saviour and it's the only one I need. The time-consuming intricacy of the labour was a form of meditation. The Mahjee collaborated closely with Marco Polo on the artwork. Charles P. Puddlejumper came out to play at the markets once a week where I was forced to engage with strangers or face the prospect of starving. I'd gone hungry too many times during my great pilgrimage and at university so I wasn't willing to exercise that option if I could help it.

Along the way I was adopted by a smooth-talking charlatan who slyly wheedled his way into my life and promoted himself to business partner. I called him Dirty Dick. It was the name of the character he played at a local theatre restaurant. He used to say it was a role not a con-dition; and he'd always laugh at the joke no matter how many times he repeated it. I didn't need any help with the market stall. I was doing fine. But Dirty saw me as an easy mark. It wasn't long before he was skimming my profits in return for the barest minimum contribution to the business.

Feeble was extremely intimidated by this man. He was ten years older than me and he was a breathtaking manipulator of the highest order. He was far more skilled than anyone I'd ever met before. In a few months my profitable business was turning a loss even though I was working harder and selling more t-shirts than ever before.

It's quite remarkable how life has led me on to new experiences. If I hadn't met Dirty Dick I wouldn't have been lifted to the next adventure in my life. Not every dunny has a silver lining, but this one most certainly did.

At some point Dirty introduced me to a woman he knew who was a literary agent. I sold her some t-shirts and she gave me her business card. I threw it in a drawer and thought nothing more of it. It was like a seed thrown down on the fertile soil. While I was off distracted by other things it began to sprout.

At last Marco Polo and the others stood up to this petty bully who'd been thieving my profits. Like all bullies, he turned out to be a coward. At the first whiff of confrontation Dirty vanished. I was overjoyed to be rid of him and I never again trusted anyone who laughed at their own jokes.

It was hard work staying inspired about my business after that. Everything that had happened to me in the previous few years was beginning to crowd in around me. I was feeling suffocated. I realised I was simply too naïve to survive in business without help. I found out I was also being ripped off by other stall-holders at the market and I was feeling very down.

The Mahjee was desperate for peace and a contemplative life. He resented the weekly trek across the city in the wee hours of the morning to set up a stall. He began demanding the solitude he'd been promised before I went to university.

In the next week everything changed for me. I dreamed about the flaming gum tree three evenings in a row. In the middle of the night Nanna vividly appeared before me and simply mouthed one word: farewell. At the next market I bumped into a cousin who told me she'd passed away the very evening I'd dreamed about her.

I was deeply grieved that I'd been forbidden to say good-bye to her. The injustice stung me. My cousin warned me not to contact any of the family. No one wanted to know about me. Father had spread the infection of his bitterness far and wide. I still believed I deserved to be ostracised. I was defective, an embarrassment, a retard and worse than an animal. Father's words came back to me again and again, 'If you were a dog we would've shot you.'

I was ashamed of myself for merely being myself. The way I'd been treated by Mother, Father, the students in my classes at university, Cheese and my Catholic teaching colleagues seemed reasonable. After all I was a psycho, a freak. There was no other explanation for their behaviour toward me. Why would people treat me so badly if I didn't deserve to be punished? Why would I be alone in the world if I was actually worth anything to anyone?

Puddlejumper was thinking about suicide again. He could see no future for me in a world where no one could be bothered to stand by me and where I had no intrinsic value except as an easy mark for conmen and thieves. I've never been interested in money. I couldn't see the point of living just to pay the rent and keep myself fed.

I've never been afraid of death. I've always known and accepted that I would die one day and that I would be alone when it happened. I began to plan my own passing and it gave me a great deal of peace to think it would soon be over. I thought about Nanna-Father and something she said to me: 'Death is not departure; it is arrival. It's not falling asleep; it is awaking. Life is the night, and death is daybreak into the world of the spirits.'

I didn't want to cause a fuss or put anyone out. I decided the best way would be to wander off into the bush and allow thirst and starvation to take me. An hour or so train ride from where I was living lay a vast forest wilderness that was largely unexplored and rarely visited, even by the park rangers who managed it.

I was winding up my affairs when I met a woman who passionately adopted me, as so many had done before. I got caught up in her world of fast cars and credit cards. I glimpsed a glimmer of hope. She drove a red sports car. I called her Red.

Red flattered me. She bought me lavish gifts. No one had ever bought me gifts before unless they wanted to bribe me. She didn't seem to want anything in return. She spoke of spending Christmas together. I hadn't shared Christmas with anyone in years. The Woman of the Red Sports Car certainly made an impact. However, as it turned out, she was using me to escape her own family and I believe she had very little real feeling for me. But if it hadn't been for her arrival just at that time I would have surely succumbed to Charles P. Puddlejumper's eloquent arguments and let him lead me off into the bush. A few months went by during which time I began to believe that someone cared for me after all. Then Red announced she was going overseas for six months on an extended holiday. Our relationship was to be put on hold. I knew Red was trying to let me down easily.

Puddlejumper teased me, 'I told you so,' he sang over and over, under my breath. Feeble was utterly exhausted from the burden of shame I'd been carrying around with me. Marco Polo felt there was nothing more I wanted to learn from the world. I'd grown tired of travelling and trying to second guess the ever-changing rules. All the knowledge I'd gathered seemed worthless and useless. I'd achieved nothing with my life. I was just another mindless consumer locked into the habit of getting money then spending it. The psychologists of my teenage years had been right. I was never going to amount to anything.

The Mahjee was the only one who refused to give up. He wasn't finished with the pilgrimage. There were still holy places to visit and shrines to kneel before. 'Pray,' he urged Marco. 'Pray,' he told Puddlejumper. 'Pray, to be granted a means to make amends for the terrible sins you have committed.'

'I'm unworthy,' Feeble argued. Then he went on to parrot back everything I'd been told about myself for years.

'Become a new person,' the Mahjee pressed. 'Show the world that you can be a good person. You did it once before when you were a boy. You can do it again. Offer the best parts of you to the world. If Pop could change his name and his identity, why can't you? This may be your last chance.'

He insisted it was time to take radical action. One night during meditation he presented the plan to me that he'd originally come up with after my encounter with the *gitanos*. 'Be the man you always wanted to be,' he whispered. 'Reinvent yourself. Rebuild the house of your soul.'

Marco Polo was suddenly inspired. This could be a chance to put all his learning to good use. What better cause is there than the redemption of a lost soul? Puddlejumper remained sceptical as usual but he agreed to go along with the others if he could be guaranteed a role in the process. He didn't want to be left out.

I closed the curtains and lapsed into three days of deep meditation. In that powerful trance I rocked endlessly back and forth searching for an answer to my dilemma. It's one thing to decide to reinvent yourself. It's quite another to actually do it.

I had no one to guide me so I had to come up with the answers all by myself. I was forced to draw on all my extensive experience of life. Actually I was very fortunate I had nobody close to me at the time. If I'd had to conform to the ways of other people, I probably wouldn't have been able to go through with it. I'd have been left with no choice but to end my life if I'd had to follow mainstream wisdom, rules or advice. In the end I actually *did* have to end my life, in a manner of speaking. If I was to move on, I came to the conclusion I couldn't allow any vestige of the old me to survive.

The former self who'd been atrophied by grief, guilt and shame, and splintered into four parts by ridicule, trauma and sorrow, breathed his last during those few days. While I isolated myself from the world and my characters sat vigil in the darkness, he passed away to a place where there was no pain.

The person I had been for 33 years was laid to rest in a tomb deep within a metaphorical crypt that would stand in the heart of the new house of my soul. Puddlejumper, Marco Polo and Feeble were his solemn pallbearers. The Mahjee spoke the final words of farewell over his grave. They buried him with great dignity and much weeping. When the grave was filled with dirt, I inscribed the name of that poor unfortunate boy upon a marble slab and solemnly vowed I would never ever make mention of him by name again. He was like one of the Pitjantjatjara people who had gone to the Dreamtime, whose name could never be uttered lest he be summoned back from the land of spirits.

Around the tomb my characters busily set about laying the foundations of a new structure. The new soul-house was rooted in an overwhelming desire to be a good, strong, generous person. The framework of the building was cut from sacred timbers that had been gathered on the great pilgrimage. The nails were fashioned from the self-discipline of spiritual practices and Tantra. The languages I'd learned and the stories I'd heard helped me to design the architectural plans for my new self. And the desire to stay safe gave me the idea to build the walls of my strong-house out of the most solid materials available. I had to be protected.

When the work was done, I found I'd built a white castle tower surmounted with battlements. It was a stronghold worthy of the Holy Grail. This new self I'd constructed was a great stone fort like one from the ancient stories I'd heard in Ireland. I made a past, present and future for this new identity that would leave the old me to rest in peace and not stir him from his grave.

The day after I emerged from my meditation I went to the registry office. In less than ten minutes I had my name officially changed to a Gaelic language phrase that meant 'great stone fort'. And that is how Caiseal Mór came into existence.

I spent the next few months constructing a history, genealogy and full characterisation for Caiseal Mór, what I called a fictional account of my life. I needed to shed the past but there were some things I couldn't discard very easily. The trauma of my young life, for example, was one aspect I couldn't simply toss aside. So I worked it into the story of Caiseal.

I felt I had to explain my aptitude for music. At university I'd been persecuted by classmates because music came so naturally to me. I felt I'd strike problems if people realised I'd had no training at all and that I'd taught myself everything I knew. A musical genealogy was very important to me. Other aspects of Caiseal such as the storytelling ability and my knowledge of languages were explained away by inventing a family that was radically different from the one I'd really been lumbered with.

When I first set out to do this I'd never thought of becoming a famous author. I just wanted to fix the problems with my life by stepping aside from myself for a while. I thought I'd be able to heal the splits by discarding all the bad things I'd been brainwashed into believing about myself.

As I look back now I can see that some people might be upset with me for presenting myself as something I'm not. I'm not trying to excuse my decision to reinvent myself, but it must be remembered that at the time I was shut down and in deep shock. Perhaps I could have done it all so much better.

The trouble was that I was completely dysfunctional and I was caught up in a dissociative identity episode. I deeply regret any hurt I may have caused by misrepresenting myself. I wish I'd been aware of what I was doing. If I'd had some guidance from someone, anyone at all, I probably wouldn't have set out on this perilous path. It's only with hindsight that I can now look back and understand that what I did was wrong. My reinvention was supposed to help me deal with shame but it has become a new source of shame for me.

I was steadily growing more out of touch with the world every day. I was descending into a state of utter panic and despair and yet, strangely, I was about to enter the most creative phase of my life.

> *All truth passes through three stages. First, it is ridiculed. Second, it is violently opposed. Third, it is accepted as self-evident.*
> (Arthur Schopenhauer, 19th-century German philosopher)

I experienced three distinct stages before I took the step of reinvention. First, I fought the idea of reinvention. I had long considered changing my identity but it was such a dangerous step to take. I'd laugh at myself for being so naïve as to believe such a simple act could heal my troubles. After Red left, Puddlejumper reasoned that suicide was preferable to reinvention. If I'd listened to him I probably would have destroyed myself. Now I know I took the best option available to me.

Mere words cannot convey to you the incredible exhilaration that accompanied my rebirth as a new person. It was truly as if I'd been reborn – the same spirit in a new body. I immediately began writing this story down so I wouldn't forget any of it – the history of my former self.

I'd made a decision that I didn't want to be poor any longer. I wanted to know what it was like to be well-off. So I applied for several jobs. I was asked to an interview as a call centre operator for a telecommunications company. In the interview I was asked whether I had any unfulfilled ambitions in life. I replied that I'd always wanted to be a writer.

I'd never really thought much about writing up to that point. When I was 18 Tantrika took me to see a Chinese fortune-teller. He'd told me I'd better learn how to type because I was going to write many, many books and that people all over the world would love my work and speak my name with fondness. At the time I thought he was stark raving mad but his incredible prediction was about to start coming true, at least in part.

My rich voice and actor training came in very handy during the job interview. I was offered a position starting a month later. When I got home I rummaged around for the business card of the literary agent I'd met six months earlier.

She must have thought I was a raving bloody loony. I rang and told the agent I'd changed my name and my life and that I had a book she might be interested in. The trouble was, I didn't. Once I'd arranged an interview with her I panicked. I couldn't believe I'd dropped myself in at the deep end. I didn't want to ruin my chances at being a writer but I sensed the time was right.

I meditated on it, and prayed, and when I emerged from my little walk in the Far Country I realised my characters were working together in a way I'd rarely experienced before. They'd surrendered their individual identities to each become a part of Caiseal. They were sheltering in the great stone fort they'd built. I later found I could still invoke them as separate entities if I needed specific advice, but they no longer jostled for position with one another.

By chance I stumbled over the journal of stories I'd collected in Ireland over ten years earlier. I bought an old Mac computer and a cheap printer for $100 and I began writing the opening chapters of my first novel. I also designed a few folios of my first non-fiction book, *Scratches in the Margin*. This was a collection of traditional Irish proverbs I'd picked up, interspersed with short stories.

The agent was immediately interested in the novel I'd begun. She asked me to come back to her with eight chapters. I went away and spent my remaining three weeks furiously writing. I sent them to her the day I started my new job.

Three weeks after I'd given her the chapters she rang to say two publishers were interested in my novel, Pan Macmillan and Random House. She advised me to go with Random House. Shortly afterwards I signed a three-book deal, got paid an advance and I was given six months to finish my first novel.

I moved closer to Sydney. I quit my job to devote all my time to writing. Red got wind of my success and flew home to Australia in a flash. She moved in with me in Sydney and I supported her for a while until she was ready to get a job of her own.

I composed and recorded an album of music to go with my first novel, but because my publisher and agent thought it would distract book-buyers from the novel they tried to prevent its release. When the first novel took off, the musicians I'd worked with on the album turned greedy and demanded bigger shares of the profits. They threatened to sue me if I didn't comply with their demands. I gave in. I didn't care about money. Profit wasn't my motivation at all. As far as I was concerned I was taking this great opportunity to heal all the hurt I'd caused throughout my life. This was my chance to make amends for being born a little bastard. I thought I'd become a moth but I was just changing into a chrysalis.

As it happened, the musicians I'd worked with kept asking for more and more. Every time I conceded a larger share to one, the others would insist on getting a bigger slice of the pie. It looked like I wasn't going to end up owning my own work. These were the first vultures to come circling around the great stone fort.

Within a year I'd finished three novels. My first, *The Circle and the Cross*, was a bestseller almost immediately. It got rave reviews all over Australia. I set up a website and I was getting 300 hits a week. This was back when the web was slow and clunky.

My old harp began falling apart due to poor workmanship. I had the plans for a new harp and I found someone who could help me build it. I didn't have the skills at woodwork and I knew I wouldn't have time to learn them while I was concentrating on writing. We agreed on a price for his services and in the meantime I was furiously composing new music for another album.

It soon became apparent to my helper that I was desperate to get the harp finished so I could begin recording the new compositions. He put up the price for his services citing demand and supply as his reasons. I didn't care how much it cost me. I just wanted to play music and I wanted this harp I'd designed to be at the centre of my life where a partner should have been. My connection with Red wasn't strong at that time. Perhaps I sensed she wasn't going to be around long.

There were countless delays in the building process, each followed by a demand for more money. The woodworker spent a lot of time in the pub. I was losing heart. Eventually I cancelled the project and told him I'd finish the harp myself. A fortnight later he helped me complete it before adding a further demand for more money.

I didn't argue. Money means nothing to me. All that mattered was I had my precious harp. I buried myself in the composition of music, poetry and stories. I played the harp six or seven hours a day; worked on my novels another ten and slept six or seven hours at most. A year or so later his dodgy work began to fall apart. I took the harp apart and put it back together. I should have trusted myself to build it in the first place.

My publicity schedule was stepped up because I appeared to be very good at public speaking and I have a strong stage presence. The harp was very popular with audiences, radio programmes and television producers. Three years at theatre school were paying off at last.

Charles P. Puddlejumper and Marco Polo loved all the publicity. But the attention soon became too much for Feeble. I'd been interviewed on television and attended a lot of book-signings. My face was becoming fairly well known. Strangers were approaching me in the street as if they knew me. I could have handled it all if I'd had someone by my side who was willing to give me the support I needed. I had no family and Red certainly wasn't up to the task. She was busy playing out her own agenda.

As soon as we'd been living together 12 months she suddenly moved out and demanded a half share of all my earnings. I'd dedicated all my books to her. I thought she loved me and that we'd always be together. We'd talked about having children. I'd felt almost normal with her. I was shattered.

Chameleon Feeble looked out over the battlements of the stone fort and he was utterly dazed by what had happened. I couldn't believe Red could walk out on me so easily. It was inconceivable to me that she'd planned it all along because I simply don't think that way and don't expect others to either. But she'd obviously seen how naïve I was right from the start. I'd built my strong tower with an eye on an external threat. But my defences had been breached from within.

By then people who should have been taking good care of me were mocking me behind my back and waiting for their chance to plunder my treasury. Folks who claimed to have my best interests at heart were manipulating me into handing over my earnings or lending them the funds to get on with their own projects. I had no one on my side to warn me to be careful.

An e-mail arrived from a cousin stating bluntly that Father had passed away from a heart attack. He'd left me out of his will. He never forgave me for ruining his life and stealing his wife away from him before her time. His funeral had already taken place by the time I found out. I was not told where he was buried and all my e-mails, begging information were afterwards ignored. The family have never forgiven me to this day for being me.

I heard Red had been having a string of affairs in the last few months we were together and that stung me even more. Naturally I blamed myself for being such a difficult bastard to get on with. I entered a period of deep remorse for being a retard. While I was distracted by the emotional fallout after Red's betrayal a few other wily brigands sneaked in the door of the castle and my once overflowing coffers were completely emptied.

One day I woke up to the realisation that I had no money, my credit cards had been picked clean and I had a tight deadline on a new book. It was the last straw for me. I shut down completely for almost six weeks; hardly eating or sleeping. I wrote furiously, spoke to no one and, as it turned out, nobody even noticed I was missing in action.

When I finally emerged from the dark closet of remorse the four parts of me were forced to take turns at the helm of Caiseal Mór for a while. I gradually descended in a deep spiral of depression. During this period I did some very eccentric things.

I wandered the streets near where I lived collecting cast-off pieces of furniture and timber off-cuts from building sites. I was putting them together in my head like a jigsaw puzzle. When I'd collected all the parts I needed, I set about building a magnificent double bed. I must have learned something watching my helper while he put the harp together.

Out of the blue I got a phone call from a business colleague. She was in a meeting with my publisher and she wanted to clarify some details of a contract. Ten minutes after the conversation she called again. She must have bumped her phone and accidentally redialled my number. She didn't realise I could hear every word she said.

At first I yelled into the phone to try to get her attention but after a few minutes I was listening with interest and mounting horror. I was so shocked by the derogatory things she said about me that tears were rolling down my cheeks. I realised she'd twigged that I couldn't understand accounts or money and that there was something disturbingly different about my approach to life. She mentioned the word 'schizophrenic'. She said I lived in a world of my own.

Up to then I'd had no idea it was so clearly apparent I was traumatised but I'd never considered the possibility I might be schizophrenic. I was deeply concerned. Like most people I had a very superficial understanding of the word. All I knew was that it was a very, very bad thing to be.

My self-esteem plummeted. I was deeply ashamed that someone could say such awful things about me. The fact that she never let on her true opinions to my face confirmed for me my worthlessness. I couldn't bring myself to confront her about that call. I tried to force the incident out of my mind but I could find no peace. Finally, after a week of agonising over the phone call, I went to a psychologist and explained the situation.

'I was diagnosed as autistic,' I told him. 'But people are saying I'm schizophrenic. I want to know the truth and I want you to tell me right now.'

He laughed at me. I swear, he laughed. I was so upset by that I had tears rolling down my cheeks. I thought he was mocking me. It turned out he was laughing because it was obvious to him by the way I'd presented myself so directly that I was autistic. Nevertheless, to satisfy my need to know the truth and have it confirmed he interviewed me about my life and I told him everything; including the invention of Caiseal.

As soon as I had a professional opinion stating that I certainly wasn't schizophrenic, I felt much better. The psychologist cautioned me about taking Caiseal too far, but I thought I could keep a lid on things. At that time post-traumatic stress disorder wasn't as widely understood as it is today. He couldn't predict what challenges I might face in the future.

My literary agent was well aware that I'd changed my name. She first met me before I became Caiseal and I never made any secret of the change. My publishers also knew. However, some boffin in the publicity department decided to make more of my invented life history. Soon I was reading publicity blurbs that had been written by people who'd never met me or even read one of my books. I was being interviewed on radio by journalists who'd take me aside before we went on air. They'd whisper that their researcher had prepared some questions for them and they'd beg me not to let on that they hadn't actually read my books. Then we'd go on air and they'd tell their listeners they'd just finished reading my latest novel. There were lies everywhere.

It was a bizarre experience to have my past created for me by strangers who hadn't really done their homework. Lazy researchers invented things about Caiseal that I couldn't possibly have dreamed up. The journalists who sculpted Caiseal Mór's past were some of the best fiction writers around at the time. It really wasn't a healthy experience for me to read some of the rubbish they wrote about me. It was on the cards that someone in my position was going to be adversely affected by all that bogus attention.

The publishers didn't seem to mind whether my past was invented or not. My books were selling very well and that's all they cared about. I expressed my concerns to various business contacts in the industry who advised me not to say anything to anyone. One business acquaintance advised me to enjoy it all while it lasted. Everything was going to turn out for the best, she promised. I had good karma, she assured me.

I'd come so far despite my autism and all my weirdness. I felt I'd begun to repay the world for being born a bastard. But the situation was rapidly getting out of hand. I had no control over my own life story and identity. No matter how much I tried to set the record straight, my protests were ignored or muffled. The myth had already outgrown the man.

I decided to set to work again on my autobiography. I wasn't ready to discuss autism with anyone as yet. I'd kept that a secret so long I simply couldn't blurt it out to everyone. In the back of my mind I still feared that I'd be institutionalised.

I spoke to friends and audiences about my experience of post-traumatic stress disorder brought on by Mother's beatings. I set about explaining my life to people. Most folks listened politely. However, behind my back, friends reckoned I was only after attention or looking for sympathy. Of course no one had the guts to tell me to my face what they truly thought of me. In time I gave up trying to tell people the truth. It was obvious no one was interested in the real me.

In the meantime I made a lot of money that was steadily siphoned into the bank accounts of others. Naïveté is a major part of who I am. It's a significant factor in my life. I struggled to understand what was happening to me because I would never dream of stealing from someone else. I tried to withdraw into my tower, but more and more people were gaining access to my life all the time. The word had got out that I was a soft touch and that I had no one to look out for me.

Some of the strange situations I got into confused me even more. For example, I was asked to launch a new fantasy novel for a first-time author at a Sydney bookstore. I arrived early to set up my harp and run through a sound check. One of the staff handed me a glass of wine and I stood pretending to sip it while the audience was assembling. A young woman and her male companion approached and struck up a conversation with me. I've always been uncomfortable with strangers but I couldn't manage to get away from them. The man suddenly started going on and on about how wonderful Caiseal Mór was. It was surreal. Didn't he know he was talking to Caiseal? Apparently not. He went on to describe me as a balding, fat, middle-aged man who nevertheless exuded a startling charisma. At least he got the middle-aged part right. He claimed Caiseal Mór was the chief druid of a secret druidic conclave.

'If it's a secret conclave how do you know about it?' Charles P. piped up, cheekily.

The young man thought for a moment then he went on to insist it was common knowledge that Caiseal was an accomplished practitioner of an ancient discipline of arcane magic. He was clearly put out that I'd challenged his word.

Feeble was beginning to shiver with fright but Puddlejumper couldn't resist throwing in a mischievous comment, 'I've heard he's a gifted shape-shifter, as well.' Charles P. wasn't much help when it came to reining in the rumours. Feeble bit my tongue to keep Puddlejumper quiet.

The young man agreed enthusiastically, adding that Caiseal was a master of the Old Ways, whatever they may be. I realised he'd been saying all this stuff simply to impress the young lady on his arm. I decided I'd better tell him who I was before he made a complete fool of himself.

Before I could utter a word he'd sprouted a pile of nonsense about my harp being 800 years old. As he finished gushing, the manager of the bookstore approached and said to me, 'We're ready for you, Caiseal.'

The young woman's jaw dropped as she looked from me to the young man and back again. Then her expression changed from admiration for her companion to absolute disgust. I can only guess what passed between them afterwards but I noticed they weren't in the audience when I was giving my speech.

If I had the space and I wasn't so embarrassed by all the situations that arose I could tell you at least a dozen incidents like that. Caiseal had expanded way beyond the bounds I'd originally set for him. I began to feel like I was the well-meaning man who'd misused the sacred words of Jesus and raised a hungry lion. I was being devoured by the monster I'd brought to life.

The eyes only see what they want to and a tree will grow much better if you pile fertiliser around the roots. In Caiseal's case, publicists and journalists provided some of the finest quality bullshit available and they spread it everywhere. The rumour-mill composted the rest. In the end the Caiseal-tree stood tall, but I was constantly on the lookout for lightning strikes.

When I realised Caiseal Mór was more popular than the old me could have ever hoped to be, I sank to a new depth of depression. I'd always known I was worthless. The Caiseal phenomenon proved that without a doubt. A fictional character I'd created to help me heal my splintered self was attracting more positive comments than I'd ever had in my life.

I've heard it argued that without Caiseal I could never have been a writer and spread so much joy to so many people. That's just one aspect of the situation. In fact, most of the praise Caiseal received was actually very superficial.

I still lived almost entirely alone because no one really cared for the real me at all. Those who claimed to be my friends were really only after a slice of the pie. Those few who saw through the mist of mythology surrounding me also saw a chance to make a killing at my expense.

A man with many cows does not sleep easy.
(Old Irish proverb)

I somehow managed to keep writing through this period, spurred on by the hope that I was creating something joyful in this world. Indeed, writing books probably saved my life. I took refuge in Caiseal Mór. I withdrew into my fort. I was so lost and confused I actually started to believe the myths that were circulating about me.

Before I could haul up the drawbridge one last time an enemy laid siege to my world. This particular attack was so vicious and unrelenting it led to the worst breakdown I've ever experienced.

It so happened that one day I had the misfortune to be introduced to a strange woman. She was the friend of an acquaintance and I was told she was a huge fan of my work. She was drunk at midday and she was loudly lamenting her stalled career as an artist. She spoke with such bitterness about the failures of her life that I named her simply Bitter.

Right from the first moment I felt there was something distinctly odd about her. I don't mean odd in an interesting way; I'm talking about odd in an unsettling, perhaps even dangerous, way. It was a brief introduction; the conversation lasted no more than a few minutes. At the time I didn't pay her too much attention because she didn't impress me at all.

I was doubting my instincts at that stage. I had been meeting so many people I was simply overwhelmed by the masses of sensory information pouring in. I won't even mention my emotional confusion, except to say I was barely holding myself together. The Flood was too much for me. One of my stronger characters often had to step forward and take over for me so I could keep going when shut-down threatened.

It was a strange period of my life. Most of the folks I felt uncomfortable about appeared to be my friends. I've said this before, if someone was friendly toward me they were also my friend. I worried I was being unjust by holding back and being less than completely accepting of my friends. I didn't want to turn paranoid just because I'd overheard one conversation I wasn't supposed to. So I convinced myself to be more open with people. I always found fault with myself before I listened to my intuition and questioned the motives of others.

This new approach was soon put to the test. Every now and then I'd bump into the strange woman when I was out shopping. I'd go into a bookshop and Bitter would be there browsing. I'd hop on a bus and she'd get on at the next stop. One night I heard someone going through the rubbish bins in the street outside. I thought nothing of it. I should've recognised the signs. Without realising it I'd attracted a stalker.

About a month after the bins had been rustled I received an unusual, unsigned e-mail professing undying adoration. It was dripping with compliments and coy flirtatious comments. My instincts screamed at me to be careful, but I laughed the whole thing off as a silly prank and didn't bother replying.

The second e-mail a few days later was more urgent. There was an edge to it that sent cold shivers down my spine. I felt a definite twinge of fear. The anonymous admirer told me she looked forward to seeing me every day. Around that time I noticed someone was going through my bin each week – usually in the middle of the night.

By then I'd become a recluse – an extreme recluse. I'd stopped all publicity and book-signings with the excuse that I had deadlines to meet. The truth was I couldn't face the bogus publicity that had been circulated about me. I used to go for weeks without speaking to anyone unless I was absolutely forced to socialise. Post-traumatic jitters will do that to you.

Though I've lived most of my life consciously confronting fear, I was feeling very vulnerable at that time. I'd become a famous author quite quickly without being properly prepared for the consequences of fame or the wiles of the media-machine that sold my story and my books. I was receiving a couple of hundred e-mails a week from readers. It was simply all too much for me.

The trickle of anonymous e-mails became a flood until there was a steady stream of ten or twelve a day. I had no idea who was writing them – I hadn't put two and two together. Within a short period they became obsessive, deeply personal and overtly sexual – all of which made me feel very uncomfortable and put me on edge.

Inevitably an e-mail finally went too far. The writer implied that I was involved in a sexual relationship with her and that I had responsibilities to that relationship. The next one added a hint of threat. I stopped reading the e-mails.

Meanwhile, Bitter turned up at the supermarket and the dentist surgery. I'd run into her at the park or the library. She was there when I played the harp for a meditation workshop at the Mind, Body, Spirit Festival in Sydney. To cut a long story short, one night I arranged to meet some friends at the movies. When I turned up, Bitter was sitting on the steps of the theatre as if she'd been waiting for me. Later that evening, after the movie, she followed me around trying to make conversation but I managed to avoid her and slip away home.

That same night as I was reading in bed by candle-light I heard a noise outside my house. The bin was being rummaged again. Puddle-jumper was outraged. He pushed the others aside and sprang into action. By the time I got to the front door all was silent again but on the opposite side of the street there was a car parked with its engine idling. In the driver's seat was the strange woman I knew as Bitter. It was mid-summer but my skin turned cold like the moment the *gitano* pulled his knife on me in the taxi in Morocco. My heart literally stopped and my hand went to my chest as I felt a sharp pain.

In a few seconds I pieced everything together. I can be terribly slow on the uptake. It's the most annoying thing about being me. I had to lean on the front door so my knees didn't give way. Bitter looked across at me, smiled sweetly, then screeched her tyres and sped off up the street.

I shut my front door, deadlocked it and sat up the rest of the night wondering what I could do. I replied to the last e-mail. I begged to be left alone. But that only made things worse. More e-mails began arriving, sometimes twenty in one hit. My reply had somehow cemented Bitter's strange obsession, perhaps making the fantasy more real to her.

Now I'm in no position to criticise anyone for enjoying a fantasy; after all, I write fantasy novels, and Caiseal Mór is a species of fantasy himself. But, as far as I was concerned, she was going too far by trying to force her way into my life. At the prompting of the Mahjee I decided to move house. I abandoned the city and found a secluded place in the mountains west of Sydney. I hoped to start afresh.

I was careful to conceal my address and keep my phone number private. I was shaky and nervous for months afterwards. The e-mails continued to come in, though less frequently, until only a short while ago when I finally changed my e-mail address.

In the mountains I had a completely different life. For the first time in years I was left almost completely alone. Agents and publishers didn't call me so much because they had to pay long-distance charges. I was being allowed to slip out of the loop. It was a great relief.

I filled the moat with dank stagnant water, closed the drawbridge and made myself comfortable in the great stone fort. In my spare time I practised the harp, composed new melodies, studied Old Irish manuscripts and esoteric works of the Middle Ages. The Holy Grail once again became the focus of my attention.

Even with all my defences up and my life dedicated to writing novels, stories filtered through to me from the outside world. Folks who had presented themselves to me as friends turned sour on me when the money ran out. I drove them out of my mind and tried to get on with my work.

At the time I was too traumatised by my experiences with Red, Bitter and the other vultures in my life to know what was right or wrong or even which way to turn. I tried to settle myself and find some calm but I couldn't relax completely.

Then without warning I experienced one of the strangest episodes in my life. One afternoon I was seated at my desk working furiously on the latest novel. I re-read a passage, made a correction, sipped my coffee and took a deep breath, closing my eyes.

The next instant I was standing outside a bookstore in a noisy city. For more than ten minutes I stood on the street mystified about what was going on. To my dismay I found I couldn't understand a word that was written on the billboards or shops. I was in a foreign country. I didn't recognise any landmarks or people.

A wave of panic struck me as I considered the possibility I'd wandered off from my carer and got lost in the crowds. The only thing I knew for certain was that I was a retarded simpleton. I didn't know what to do. Eventually I decided the best thing for me was to wait where I was. Whoever was looking after me had a better chance of locating me if I stayed put.

Then, in a blinding flash everything suddenly fell back into place. I'd been thinking in German. As soon as English returned to me I knew exactly where I was. I could read the street signs and billboards. I knew I was in Sydney 150 kilometres away from my home. I caught a bus to the railway station and then I took the two-hour train journey back to the mountains.

When I got home my cup of coffee was still by the keyboard of the computer and the cursor was still flashing in front of the last word I'd typed. I've never been able to work out how I got so far from home without some memory of the journey.

As winter approached, lapses like that were happening more and more frequently, though few were as dramatic. I was nervous about the time I seemed to lose but I was unwilling to allow it to distract me from my work. In the back of my mind I believed that my inevitable end was not far off and that I would soon be relegated to the mental home. I'd lock myself in the house and tie myself to the chair so I couldn't wander off as easily.

I'd felt relatively safe in my home in the mountains until my perceptions started playing tricks on me. I was almost completely alone by that stage so I was probably not taking it all very well. After the lapses began I became more and more unsettled. I don't like being ruled by fear. I've usually stood up to it whenever I've caught a whiff of its stench. One day I looked out over the battlements I'd built for myself and I decided to make a stand.

I realised I'd achieved a degree of independence that would have been unimaginable for me once. Royalties were still rolling in; I was about to sign a new book deal; the weekly struggle to get the rent together and feed myself was a thing of the past.

I enthusiastically took up Sufi dancing in the privacy of my home. I meditated long hours. I sang songs of thanks to God for the freedom I'd been granted. I spent more time drumming, creating poetic accompaniments to my spiritual journey and walking by myself in the great wilderness of the Blue Mountains.

There was always so much to do. I hurried eagerly about my pursuits with a sense of very real urgency, exhausting myself so that I fell into bed each night and slept. No matter how tired I was I never slept soundly. My body collapsed every night but my dreams were not quiet or restful. I was stuck in the Near Country. The burning gum tree was always present in my mind. I suffered terrifying visions of the past interwoven with the future. I felt like a ship adrift without a rudder in a terrible storm.

In this manner I spent the next six years of my life. I completely forgot the old me during that time. I stopped visiting his tomb in the depths of my tower. I utterly lost myself in the strange misty veil of amnesia that swept over me. I can recall only a few specific events that happened during that period. I don't know what became of the money I earned or the people who flitted in and out of my life.

I know I went to the UK on a publicity tour in 1999, but I have very little recollection of what happened to me there except for my journey to Ireland. I took my harp with me and I know I played lots of music. I went to Inish Mor in the Aran Islands and there I composed a wonderful piece of music as I sat out by the Iron Age hill fort of Dun Aonghusa. I also met a few Australians I knew in London. One of them was soon to become my UK publisher.

I don't remember much of four of the novels I wrote during those years. I haven't got the faintest idea what any of them is about. I can only remember parts of the latest three books I've written. I know I composed and recorded lots of music because I have six finished CDs on the bookshelf to prove it.

For some reason I haven't worked out yet, I eventually moved back to Sydney in 2001 and there my life seemed to be on the mend again. I was beginning to wake up. But I was in no state to judge whether things were going well or not. Within a few short months of arriving in the city my life had taken another drastic turn for the worse.

Eight

The first time I woke up from a lapse and realised I wasn't where I'd left myself, just a blink of the eye earlier, it pretty much freaked me out completely. I was deeply disturbed to have lost control of my thought processes. It was if my body had been used as a vessel to contain another spirit. My own spirit could only stand back in awe as the being of light took possession. This wasn't anything like the way my characters operated. I was always aware when they took control and I always remembered what had happened.

The second time I lapsed into the fog it wasn't any less disturbing an experience. But as always, my clicking mind had tried to take careful note of every little detail so it could compare the two instances. I was very confused. I had to concentrate all my will so I wouldn't collapse in panic every time a lapse occurred.

On nine major occasions that I know of, and in many minor instances, I lost generous slices of my life. By the time the last one hit I still wasn't getting used to the idea at all. On the contrary, the very thought of losing memories or, worse still, of losing myself was enough to set me on the verge of panic. What changed as the lapses went on was that I got over each little stint in the Far Country much quicker.

In the middle of the night in the summer of 2002 I sat up straight in the bed I'd made for myself out of cast-off bits of timber from building sites and construction bins. There was a breeze flowing in through the open windows and I caught a hint of the pungent scent of eucalyptus. The night was quite bright so I thought there must be a full moon. I looked around the room struggling to recall where I was and how I'd got there. I recognised all my possessions laid out on bookshelves. On my desk was a familiar computer and keyboard. Angus, the ginger cat who'd been my companion for more than 12 years, was fast asleep at my feet. But I couldn't for the life of me recall how I'd come to be in that room. When I sat up I experienced a sharp pain at the crown of my head. My eyesight blurred.

My attention was drawn to the sound of heavy traffic outside. This was confusing. I managed to drag myself to the window and look down to the street. I was on the second floor of an apartment block. There were cars banked up along the road moving at a snail's pace.

The bright lights streamed in my eyes like vivid paint smeared across a canvas. The lights suddenly began flickering. I felt dizzy. I had to support myself against the windowsill. A wave of nausea hit me. I had to struggle not to throw up.

The lights on the street took on the appearance of flames. The scent of eucalyptus grew stronger. My gum tree dream came back to me. I made my way to the bed and lay on my back. I still had no idea where I was.

I must have drifted off to sleep again. When I awoke the night was still bright. I heard a wailing siren and I got up to go to the window again. I realised it wasn't full moon at all. The brightness was coming from street lights outside. I was in the middle of a city. I couldn't work out what had happened.

The last thing I remembered I was living in a quiet street in a small country town high in the Blue Mountains. Suddenly I was in the middle of Sydney. A car raced along the road outside and pulled up suddenly opposite my window. The sirens were getting much louder. I watched a bloke swing open the driver's door of the car to step out. He'd just put a foot on the bitumen when a police car pulled up behind him. He slammed the door again and started the engine. Another police car, travelling in the opposite direction, crossed from the other side of the street to block his escape.

Guns were drawn as six police surrounded the car demanding the man get out and show his hands. In a flash he was suddenly down on the ground on his stomach with two cops on top of him. They hand-cuffed him while the other police pointed their pistols at his head. Next thing he was bundled into one of the police cars which departed immediately. The other cops turned out the car, proudly holding up a heavy shopping bag and congratulating one another.

Then they and the suspect's car were gone. I was left standing at the window for a long while. The sky was lightening in the half-hour before dawn when I finally decided to go and find out where I was.

I picked up my digital camera from the desk and a bunch of keys I recognised as my own even though I didn't know what doors they opened. I heard people talking in another room of the apartment.

I wasn't in any mood to speak with people so I sneaked out through the front door, made my way down the stairs and out on to the street. I smelled the awful pollution immediately. It gave me a terrible headache. But among the sulphur fumes and exhaust stench I detected a hint of salt like the sea.

I took a photo of the front door so I'd be able to identify it when I returned. Then I literally followed my nose along the long street outside the building. The smell of the ocean was getting stronger and stronger with every step until I saw the beach at last. From the street signs I worked out I was in Coogee, a beach suburb of Sydney. The sun was coming up over the ocean painting everything in gold, orange and red. I took a photo of the spectacular scene. Then I sat down on the deserted beach for a while to clear out my lungs. As I stood up to make my way back to the apartment I suffered another sharp pain in my head.

The next thing I remember I was lying on my back in the sand. The sun was hot and my mouth was dry. There were people all around me and a lot of noise. I shook myself, stood up and headed back to my cat.

My body was stiff and sore. I was desperately thirsty but I had no money on me to buy a bottle of water. I found the door to the apartment building by comparing all the doors to the photo on my camera. Then the strangest thing happened. The very instant I put the key in the lock I remembered everything. I knew who I was, where I was and how I'd come to be there.

★ ★ ★

I went upstairs to the apartment. My housemate was on her way out and she asked me where I'd been. I told her I went for a walk before dawn. She replied that I looked very ill and advised me to take it easy. I must have downed a litre of water before my thirst was quenched. Angus was rubbing against my leg begging for food. I went to the cupboard and found his food without thinking. It was as if a light had come on in a dark place.

I still had the most awful headache. It was right at the very centre of the crown of my head. I didn't know what to make of it. If I moved my head suddenly, my eyes lit up with thousands of tiny candles, flickering on a dark background.

I lost my balance a couple of times that day. One time the floor seemed to fly up and throw itself against me. My cheek crashed on the carpet in the lounge room where I lay paralysed for a long while staring helpless at distorted images on the television.

It was obvious something was very wrong. I just didn't want to admit it. I knew I'd had previous blackouts, but I always brushed them off as nothing to worry about. I put off going to the doctor for a few days until the agonising little lightning bursts of pain had spread to my eyes. I couldn't see clearly. My vision was blurred. I couldn't focus on anything. It was as if there was a sharp pin stuck right through each eyeball into my brain. I explained all this to the doctor.

He asked me a lot of questions as he examined my skull. He was surprised to find there were deep indentations where it had been damaged a long time ago. There's a spot at the very crown of my skull where it feels soft as if there's a hole where's there no bone covering my brain. I got frightened when he told me I must have suffered a severe head trauma as a child. I'd never noticed the scars before and Mother had never mentioned any accident to me.

I tentatively touched the places the doctor indicated were the worst spots. I felt strange ridges running along the top of my skull, fore and aft, that felt like my head had been crushed in a vice. It was shocking. I thought I'd known myself. It was like waking up in another person's body. I went home and shaved all my hair to get a better look at the damage.

I'd never noticed it before. That's strange when you consider I had a shaved head until I was ten years old. I must have always had these identifying scars. How could I have never noticed them before?

The doctors had said I was brain-damaged to begin with. I recalled that Mother had said when I was born I wasn't expected to live. I must have been in a bad way, my bare skull is fairly ugly to look at. The doctor recommended tests. I went along with it. By then I was having blackouts that were lasting for quite long periods. I dimly recall lying on my back in a big machine and being told to stay perfectly still. After a visit to a psychologist, my autism was confirmed. There was another shock in store for me. I was told I was suffering from dissociative identity disorder. Anyone reading this who knows the first thing about the condition would have probably worked that out by now.

Dissociative identity disorder (DID for short) used to be called multiple personality disorder. It was once considered to be a psychiatric illness related to schizophrenia and it was often confused with it by laymen and psychiatrists alike. These days a lot more is known about the way in which the mind deals with childhood abuse and traumatic situations.

The human mind is a fascinating thing. It has mechanisms built in to it that allow us to survive the most horrendous events by tapping into the well of our imagination. Recent research has confirmed this experience is common to many young children who've suffered repeated abuse.

I'm not a trained psychologist but this is my simple understanding of DID. I suggest you look it up on the net if you want to know more. When a child suffers ongoing abuse that is of a physical, emotional or sexual nature their reaction may be to withdraw into themselves. They may separate their conscious minds from the person who perpetrated the abuse or the place where it happened.

In some extreme cases, depending on the severity of the abuse, the child may splinter into several distinct apparent aspects or characters. These characters may continue to prevail throughout life without proper treatment. I knew and understood the Mahjee, Charles P. Puddlejumper, Marco Polo and Feeble. I just didn't understand where they'd come from before I was given that explanation. The psychologist put my mind at ease about treatment and my future was suddenly looking much brighter. I felt that with sufficient concentration on the task I'd be able to work on my problems and fix myself.

No doctor could explain my apparent head injury or tell me whether it had contributed to or caused the symptoms of autism. The theory that ended up being presented to me was that I had probably been delivered with forceps by an inexperienced or clumsy physician. Some current evidence from the UK and US appears to indicate that autistic children are more likely to have experienced a traumatic birth. I believe a forceps birth or caesarean section is very common among autistic children. It's a contentious issue. The medical profession don't like to face their mistakes and they vehemently defend their methods. But as Schopenhauer observed, truth goes through three stages, so we'll have to wait and see whether doctors ever take responsibility for their practices.

They offered me painkillers and the usual, wildly varying opinions. One specialist told me the damage to my skull could have actually been responsible for my creativity. None of them really offered any answers. It was obvious they were guessing. Eventually one doctor came to the conclusion I was suffering the onset of dementia caused by a combination of an early head injury and post-traumatic shock. He said I could expect to end up in palliative care possibly within two to three years. He advised me to settle up my affairs.

I'd heard all that before so I wasn't about to let despair get the better of me. I'd well and truly lost faith in the medical profession by that stage. I refused their medications. Ever since the Stick-Insect gave me his pills as a child, I've been suspicious of pharmaceuticals. I didn't want to be put to sleep.

I read up everything I could find about dementia and I immediately instituted measures to help slow the process. If I have a goal in my sights there's no stopping me. With renewed inspiration I took up more demanding meditation exercises, expanding my daily practice to include a physical workout and the acquisition of new skills.

One of the brain teasers I set myself was to learn a state-of-the-art computer programme for arranging musical compositions. Within six weeks I knew the programme inside out. I looked on it as a language. As a result I'm now able to produce my own music without the need for studio engineers or a producer.

Within a year I'd brought the blackouts under control through a combination of meditation, rigorous self-examination and determination. I was still writing novels and I finished the particular one I was working on in record time. I believe it was very fortunate I had something to concentrate my intellectual energies on. The novel was probably a crucial factor in staving off further deterioration of my alertness. However, the moment I finished work on it I fell into deadly peril from the most dangerous of all quarters. Boredom.

With no major direction to focus my attention I was becoming more and more anxious every day. At last Chameleon Feeble and the Mahjee fell into a bitter dispute. The spiritual part of me was urging me not to fall back into the old person I was before Caiseal Mór. The new identity was difficult to maintain when I was having lapses of time and becoming very confused.

Feeble was expressing his anxiety in strange ways. I hoarded felt-tip calligraphy pens. If I went into the city, I was compelled to buy one pen from a certain bookshop. Some days I'd make the trip to the city just because the pens made me feel so much better. A simple act like buying a pen was enough to calm my terrible anxiety but not enough to bring my emotions under control.

I used to walk sometimes ten or twelve kilometres in a morning to settle me down. I was smoking cigarettes at the time. It wasn't the smoking that calmed me down. It was rolling the cigarette with one hand that quietened my anxiety.

Worse still, Feeble was beginning to get angry about everything that had happened to me as a child. I was stirred up and frustrated. I began to have fleeting reminders of the rage attacks I'd suffered when I was a little boy.

An acquaintance at the time had built her life around the consumption of amphetamines. She somehow convinced Chameleon Feeble to give Speed a try. Eager to please, he fell for the sales pitch and took up chemicals for a while. I'd tried Speed in London years earlier but I'd only taken it to help me through double shifts at work. And the stuff I had back then wasn't very pure. My acquaintance only purchased the finest quality chemicals for her indulgences.

The first thing I noticed about Speed was that it initially calmed me down. All anxiety, agitation and anger were banished instantly. My confidence returned and I was able to look at situations objectively. But it didn't take long for me to realise there was a terrible cost for this very temporary relief. I wasn't as easily overwhelmed by sensual information. The stuff distracted my brain so I could ignore my senses if I wanted to. This effect only lasted while the drug was in my system. As soon as I'd recovered, I'd suffer massive overloads of sensory information.

Other people I knew spoke of a 'come-down' period after the drug had worn off. That could mean anything from mild depression through to incredible nausea or even suicidal rage. I was completely the opposite. Speed switched off my senses, which invariably returned with increased intensity that could last a week.

The same happened with my emotions. When I was under the influence of Speed my emotional responses were much more balanced. I was able to flow smoothly from one emotion to the next without feeling overwhelmed. However, when the drug was finished with me I'd go into a few days of such powerful emotion that I simply had to shut myself away and stay in bed. I couldn't think. I couldn't write. I couldn't hear or play music without experiencing a devastating bout of emotion that could leave me in tears or laughter. It wasn't depression. Rather, it was similar to what some folks call a mood swing. It was like being on a constantly bobbing see-saw.

While I had the stuff in my system I simply couldn't switch off my chattering mind. For someone who's used to meditating every day and being able to quieten the thought processes this was very disturbing. I probably wouldn't have been so upset if I could have turned my mind to productive pursuits. But Speed seemed hell-bent on exploring and expostulating on a wide range of useless trivia. I began to wonder if most television writers indulge in this particular drug.

My body suffered worst of all. During the tyranny of the drug I was constantly dehydrated. After it wore off, I felt as if I'd been hit by a truck. I was forced to stay awake for days by that evil rubbish. It took an incredibly long time to clear out of my body, and all the while I felt sicker than I'd ever done in my life.

I suppose Speed was as close to Ritalin as I'm ever going to experience. The outbursts of rage I'd been suffering diminished, then disappeared. By focusing the immense power of my will on productive pursuits I was eventually able to look at my life objectively without being overwhelmed by the flood of emotions that got stirred up by memories.

I began believing I was receiving valuable insights into the mystery of my life. I wrote everything down in a calligraphic script hoping I'd get some messages from my deeper being that I could act on. It was an interesting experience, but most of what I wrote was absolute rubbish that made no sense to me afterwards. Speed was a complete waste of my time. I wasn't impressed with the experience. It didn't take long for the initial, seemingly positive, effects of the drug to wear off. I thought the way to deal with this would be to raise the dose.

Then I thought again. I took a long hard look at my acquaintance and realised I didn't want to suffer as she was suffering for a very small apparent benefit. She was very ill at the time and she was experiencing disturbing side-effects.

I'm very fortunate to be in the habit of examining myself and my immediate environment from day to day. That saved me from a downward spiral into addiction. I came to the conclusion that if I lifted the dose I was in danger of becoming reliant on the stuff. The other factor that kept me safe was the same reason I'd never been able to become addicted to drugs or alcohol. I'm easily bored.

My immune system quickly collapsed under the deadly assault from this foul substance. And I wasn't taking anywhere near as much as some people I knew at that time. It's a miracle some of them were walking around at all. I stopped taking Speed and I never had it again. Nor will I.

I lost so many skills under the assault of that stuff. I put down the harp and never really picked it up again. I lost German, Gaelic and Spanish. I lost my singing voice. The drug didn't wipe my hard drive. That's not what I'm saying at all.

If I'm not passionately interested in an activity or project, I just can't pursue it. Something in me switches off. Under the influence of Speed I simply lost interest in the harp, the languages I'd learned and some of the performance skills I'd developed. In my opinion drugs like that literally steal the soul. I can attest to that first hand. Perhaps I'll eventually be able to recover interest in the lost subjects. Only time will tell.

★ ★ ★

I'd almost recovered from Speed when I contracted pneumonia and ended up in bed for a week. The drug had played havoc with my immune system. I was just getting over my lung problems when I won a contract for three fantasy novels. So I moved out into a tiny one room flat. I cut my ties with all drugs and drug users.

I wrote *The Well of Yearning* in that tiny flat. I was working 12 or 14 hours a day and I loved it. Novels are a great distraction. I love storytelling, and this book proved to be my favourite. The narrator is based on an old woman I met in south-west Ireland in the eighties. She's got a wicked sense of humour, she's worldly, well-travelled and wise. The Mahjee, Charles P. and Marco Polo all rolled into one.

Indeed the three of them were suddenly thriving on the challenge of being Caiseal Mór. The odd one out of the relationship had always been Feeble – poor frightened Chameleon Feeble. He was the weakest link, the one who could be depended on to panic or wimp-out at the last minute.

He wasn't happy with life. He kept whispering to me that I couldn't go on like this forever. It took me a while to realise that he'd been the only one of the characters who'd had anything to gain from Speed. It gave him confidence where he had none. It allowed him to come out of his shell without fear for the consequences. His jumpiness around this time confirmed for me that I should never go near amphetamines again.

While I was writing *The Well of Yearning* my agent advised me my career was at an end. She didn't feel there was enough interest in my work any more. She suggested I should make the decision to move to another way of making a living.

I was devastated. Storytelling had been my life for ten years. I'd come to identify myself as a writer. I thought I'd always be able to make a living at it. I finished the novel I was working on, then I spent six weeks intensely working at my autobiography.

I told my agent a bit about it and she showed some initial interest. She listened to me talk about post-traumatic stress and told me there might be a market for the work. However, when I revealed to her for the first time that I was autistic she advised me not to tell people in the publishing industry in case it put them off me. I put the manuscript away in a drawer and forgot all about it.

I decided I wasn't going to be brought down so I got on with recording the compositions I'd created to accompany the novel *The Well of Yearning*. I'd been working with an old friend from university days who had his own recording studio, but he'd been proving more and more difficult to motivate. I paid him large sums of money to keep him on the project. I very foolishly looked up to him and thought he was too good-hearted to cheat me. He made effusive promises about finishing the album on deadline. I was completely focused on having the CD released at the same time as the novel was published so I ignored the warning signs. I was wearing myself out.

While I was sleeping
You brought to me
Gifts of Love,
In your Beautiful Hands.
(From the song *Woman at the Well* by Caiseal Mór)

I got home from the recording studio one evening to find an e-mail from a young woman who'd just picked up one of my books. She'd written to say she was impressed at all the things we had in common. She played the lyre; I play the harp. We shared a fascination for history, 19th-century fashions and music. She was an artist, singer, photographer, performer and actor. Without too much fanfare Helen had entered my life. I knew she wasn't anything like Bitter right from the start but I was careful to keep her at a distance.

It turned out Helen has a love of costume design, particularly of the period 1860s to 1890s. I've been collecting clothes from that era for a long while. I could hardly believe she was into exactly the same things I was.

I wrote a polite reply to her lovely e-mail. I found it a strange coincidence that such an amazing person lived over a thousand kilometres away in the tropics near where I'd grown up. Over a period of three or four months we wrote to one another occasionally. But both of us were committed to our individual careers and there wasn't much room really to get to know one another. I'd long since concluded that no one would want to share my eccentric world. I'd thrown myself into my work to compensate for the emptiness in my heart. And so had she.

I got caught up in the production of the *Well of Yearning* CD and due to my extremely difficult producer-friend, progress was painfully slow. I was planning a DVD promo for the CD and the novel but I couldn't find anyone to play the female lead. Most of the actors I knew from university days either weren't interested in working for me or hadn't worked since they'd graduated from theatre school.

The day of the filming was fast approaching. My friend the producer hadn't completed the track we were intending to film. It looked like the project was going to have to be shelved. He'd sucked me dry of funds, promising to complete the mixing and mastering, but he'd done very little real work.

Just when it was looking like the whole project was doomed, I suffered a relapse of pneumonia. I was admitted to hospital in a serious condition. I awoke a week later. No one had noticed I'd dropped off the radar. Feeble was exhausted from the high levels of anxiety and stress. The Mahjee was screaming out at me to do something about the parasite producer, but I couldn't give up on the album after putting so much work into it.

I was more alone than I'd ever been in my life. I really felt I had nothing to live for and that no one would miss me if I was gone. Despite all this negativity around the project it suddenly, miraculously, came together. The producer got his act together and finished the track.

A couple of weeks before the shoot we still hadn't found an actor to play the female lead. Then out of the blue Helen rang me. She'd got worried that she hadn't heard from me in a while. We were chatting away when I realised she'd be perfect for the part. The next thing I knew I was waiting to pick her up at Sydney airport.

When she stepped off the aeroplane it was love at first sight. We recognised kindred spirits in one another. Her eyes spoke of her struggle for acceptance and I was drawn to her straightaway.

Helen was never diagnosed with autism. Recently she has spoken with a psychologist who confirmed that she has many autistic attributes and suffers the complication of post-traumatic stress. We had more in common than we could have imagined. For example; her naïveté has made her a target for predators throughout her life. And if she sets her sights on a goal, she achieves it.

However, Helen deals with the real world much better than I do. For example, she can read numbers and accounts. She can look at a bank statement and understand what it means. I find that almost unbelievable.

She really is an amazing woman, my best friend and an incredible inspiration to me. In the few years since we first met she's transformed her life completely. She's turned herself into a brilliant portrait artist with a highly successful business.

I could go on about Helen all day, but I think her story is best told in her own words. The most amazing thing about her is that she accepts me and genuinely searches for ways to deal with my difficult nature. Since we first met we've rarely strayed out of sight or sound of one another. We work well together because neither of us has ever had anyone who truly cared about us before, only fly-by-night charlatans who were after what they could get.

I've never known absolute acceptance like this, and I believe it's had a deeply healing effect on my splintered self. Over the last few years I've been able to look back on my life with a new perspective. Now that I have a better understanding of what love can mean I've come to believe that Love alone can heal all the hurt in my life.

I've found that when Love equals acceptance, support, commitment and sharing, it can have an astounding effect on the pain of the past. Helen was initially shocked that I had no one to look in on me now and then. She couldn't believe I was so isolated from the world. So she set herself the task of becoming a kind of guardian for me. She shields me from the aspects of the world I can't cope with. She could probably write a book herself on how she deals with my unpredictable, eccentric under-standing of life.

With Helen to support me I kicked the producer's arse until the album was finally wrapped up. By then Helen had convinced me to move back to Queensland with her. She'd never been too far from home and she was very uncomfortable in the big city.

With some reservations with regard to my own painful memories of the place, I agreed. We moved to the Sunshine Coast and it was then she revealed to me the appalling circumstances of her childhood. It was a bombshell. My own self-indulgent rubbish was immediately forgotten. I found myself in a position I'd never imagined I'd have to face.

Not long after we settled into our new life Helen suffered a terrible breakdown. I don't want to go into the details here. This is Helen's story to tell, not mine.

We moved away from Queensland once and for all. I pray every day that I'll never have to return to that awful place.

Under the circumstances my characters were forced to put aside their differences. They quickly agreed to a permanent truce with the Mahjee as the guiding aspect. Feeble was initially reluctant to hand over the reins to the Mahjee but the others convinced him to comply. I'd created Caiseal Mór as a means of welding my splintered selves together. It may have been misguided but it was certainly an effective way to prepare myself for further healing. What I didn't realise was that the creation of Caiseal was merely a step in the journey to wholeness.

The real catalyst for my healing was the presence in my life of Helen. I had to forget my own difficulties so I could stand by her in her hour of need.

We've been sharing our pilgrimage now for three years. In that time we've stood up to bullies and taught each other a few strategies for dealing with people who can't accept us. One of the most amazing things we've done together was to make a dream come true.

We were talking about our dreams one morning over breakfast. I mentioned that ever since I'd seen the dreaddie-woman in the street in London I'd wanted to lock my hair. I'd never acted on the desire for locks. It wasn't going to happen in the eighties, let's face it. I told her that whenever I see myself in a dream I've got long tightly knotted locks of hair.

'Why don't you get dreadlocks?' she asked.

'Why not?' I shrugged.

Helen began researching the process of locking and, being the obsessive person she is, in a short while she'd worked out how to do it. We spent three days locking my hair. It was a magical experience, a transformation and a shock.

I hadn't expected to be so comfortable with locks. I hadn't expected to feel so much like myself. I believe locks were a major step in the healing of my various parts. It's almost as if my characters are bound and woven into the tight locks where the various aspects of me are forced to remain in close proximity and co-operation. Locks have been a very potent symbol for me – a binding agent, a metaphysical glue, if you like. I'm now a much more integrated person. My characters work much better together and the transitions between their attributes and personalities are much smoother.

There are several other reasons why this transformation was important and timely for me. Up to then I'd worn my hair neatly parted on one side. It was always combed and I'd washed it every day ever since I was a child. Whenever strangers met me they thought I was a conservative-looking, mild-mannered, polite conformist. That opinion would inevitably change as they got to know me. I'm neither conservative nor conformist. I'm creative, adaptive, eccentric and adventurous. The apparent contradiction was often too much of a challenge for most people to cope with. But locked hair turned that situation around completely. The moment someone met me they could see I was different. It was like wearing a neon sign on my forehead that read – Warning! This bloke is different. I found I was suddenly more accepted. As I realised other people were very comfortable with my appearance, I became more comfortable with myself.

I also discovered that anyone who suffers the slightest prejudice doesn't usually bother with me. Confirmed bigots prefer not to be challenged. As I've said before, prejudice cannot exist without ignorance. People are often frightened by those things they don't know or understand; so it follows that prejudiced folks often avoid facing anything they're even mildly frightened of.

Not only did prejudiced people begin avoiding me; many people I already knew as friends showed their true colours. Some said I was mad; others that I was a psycho. They all sang the same old tunes I'd heard a hundred times before.

The producer-friend who'd worked for me on my music just couldn't handle the change. His partner put pressure on him not to work with me again. I couldn't believe my luck. I didn't have to push him away. He just flew off and didn't come back.

When I first met Helen, certain colleagues in the publishing game expressed disapproval of our relationship. I'd been wanting to break with some of them for many reasons but I hadn't been able to bring myself to confront them. Perhaps some of them felt the same way about me. After I had my hair locked I was told bluntly that dredlocks were unacceptable. I was informed I'd never work as a writer again.

I must admit all these reactions were an eye-opener for me. I didn't expect such anger. I wondered whether I'd gone too far. Now, however, I'm overjoyed that I locked my hair. It weeded out the parasites, the hangers on, the insincere, the opportunists and the prejudiced.

When Helen saw the profound change that came over me she locked her hair as well. We had a picture taken of us the day she got her hair done. I still look at that photograph in wonder. I can hardly believe how happy we both are. The fear and anxiety aren't completely gone, but they've certainly taken a back seat.

Since my hair was locked I've been more comfortable with sharing my experience of the dream-world; the world I call the Far Country. Without intending to, I managed to turn my visits to that otherworld into profitable forays. Ever since I started writing I've clearly dreamed the scenes, episodes and characters of my novels. Next morning all I have to do is sit down at the computer and copy down everything that happened in my dream the previous night. If I'm working intensely on a novel the story usually flows seamlessly into my dreams. Or should I say my dreams flow into my novels? I'm not certain.

The same happens with my music. It's been described by critics as cinematic, emotionally stirring, sensual and epic. I lose myself in sound when I'm composing and I often dream complete orchestrated pieces which I record first thing in the morning. Until quite recently I thought everyone could do that.

These dreaming experiences have become much more intense, satisfying and enjoyable since I had my hair locked. I suppose I've relaxed a lot. I'm not worried what other people think of me any more. To me, dreadlocks are dreamlocks. These days I'm not as ashamed as I used to be that my waking life and my dreaming experiences are seamlessly woven together.

Nine

My characters have all evolved and changed as they grew older. There was a time when Charles P. Puddlejumper was the angry one. He hated society, he hated conformity and he wanted everyone to know about it. When Caiseal came into existence Charles calmed down a lot. He's learned to revel in the pleasure of creativity and the joy of life. He actually likes to learn about other people. This is mostly due to the influence of the Mahjee.

After I became Caiseal Mór, it was Marco Polo who started to experience bouts of rage and anger. At first he begrudgingly worked with the others on creative projects. Eventually he began to enjoy his role as front-man for the Caiseal road-show. He's confident with public speaking, doesn't appear shy at first glance and copes with social chit-chat better than the rest.

However, it was Marco who first realised what I was missing out on. Family. Security. Guidance. Love. Emotional support. It was Marco who first began to glimpse that I was being exploited by unscrupulous users. Then Marco Polo began to rebel. It's only recently I've realised just how much Marco took over my life. In my splintered state I could hardly perceive what was going on. I was in a strange dream-like trance where everything seemed to be out of my control. For years Marco Polo drove many well-meaning people away with his brashness, his abruptness and his apparent arrogance.

I understand that Marco had become the most frightened of all my characters, even though he'd once been the most adventurous. These days he can't stand the company of people and he's very confronted by others.

He isn't very comfortable with admitting that I'm autistic or talking about my quirks.

I had to engage in a bitter fight with him to get this autobiography finished. In the end the Mahjee struck a deal. He promised that the pilgrimage to Morocco would be mentioned in detail. Those were Marco's glory days. It's an awful struggle to get him to come out without expressing his deep mistrust, rage and anger at others, but I'm sure he'll grow out of it.

Marco's reticence probably wouldn't be a problem if it weren't for the fact that when I feel uninspired, which is very rarely, I find I need the company of others. A single evening spent with other human beings can renew my spirit and rejuvenate my passion. A few individuals have a certain spiritual spark about them. If Marco doesn't interfere, that spark will jump across the gap between us like a static electric stinger seeking the quickest route to discharge. I consider the sparks of others to be precious. I treasure them, but I don't feel a compulsion to experience sparks all the time.

When the right set of circumstances exists and the other person is open to it, such connections are nearly always intense, healing and transforming. They may sometimes lead directly to cataclysmic changes in my life and the life of the person with whom I shared the connection. Once in a while I may even meet someone who understands and accepts me.

The moment I looked into Helen's eyes I knew she was going to be my friend. I breathed a sigh of relief to feel so safe in the presence of another human being. There have been other women in my life, but Helen is the first I've been able to trust. Helen looks after me and shows me what it is like to be looked after.

I trust her because she has told me her deepest darkest inner secrets. Helen is my heroine. I look up to her. Every day I'm amazed at how good-hearted, generous, selfless and forgiving Helen can be. I use her name a lot. I love her name.

Helen has given me time to relax and heal myself. For the first time in my life I can breathe a little easier. No one's ever done that for me before. I've never been able to be calm around others. It's nothing short of a miracle for me to feel safe. But even Helen needs me to explain some aspects of myself to her.

I can't speak to you in the diagnostic language of the medical profession. I'm not a trained psychologist. I can only explain myself to you in my own terms and hope you find some way to glimpse a meaning in what I'm saying.

I've had to work out the puzzle of my existence for myself through careful and diligent observation, by challenging my fear and by asking many questions. Over the years I've come up with a few guidelines for people who have to deal closely with me. These guidelines may offer clues on how to interact with other autistic people but please don't take them literally. In my opinion every autistic person has a completely different experience of the world.

First and most important of all – don't break my concentration. This is one of the most common causes of rage. When I'm absorbed in an activity, I'm off in the Far Country. Basically I'm meditating deeply in a completely relaxed state. Sometimes this state will be a kind of shutdown from the overwhelming stimulus of the world. More often it's an intense focus that allows me to learn skills and plan projects.

At university I was seeing a girl whose mother lived on the far side of Sydney. To visit her mother we'd have to take a train, then change buses twice. By the time I got on to the second bus I'd be so overwhelmed by the noise, sights and smells of Sydney that I'd be staring out the window in a trance. My friend was always deeply offended. She thought I was being rude to her, that I was deliberately ignoring her; but that wasn't the case. It may seem as though I'm not interested in what's going on around me or that I'm being deliberately rude.

If it happens that I drift off into the Far Country it's because I simply can't handle all the stimuli rushing at me. In extreme cases I'm so exhausted from the constant barrage of information that I get cranky, especially if I'm not allowed to rest my weary mind and body.

Let me take a break from everything for half an hour. Leave me alone to my own meditations and don't insist that I engage with the world. Certainly don't try to make small talk with me. Small talk on a trivial, superficial level is one of the things I least understand about human social interaction, and it makes me very angry. I can engage in small talk when I'm well rested and I'm in a quiet environment. But put me in a busy theatre foyer after I've been on stage for a couple of hours and I simply can't take it. I don't understand why anyone bothers with silly discussions about the weather when they really have other things on their minds.

Like most autistic people I'm fairly blunt in conversation. I find it difficult to conceal my feelings or thoughts. I believe in honesty in conversation. If I detect someone is hiding something from me I can become very agitated. This is possibly because Mother had a habit of teasing me with treats but following it up with a thrashing.

I can't understand why people beat around the bush. I know they get frightened, but so do I. Yet I manage to push on past it. I'm told that because I've been exposed to a lot more fear on a daily basis as a young child than most people I may have become desensitised to it. What I consider little fears may be huge hurdles to other people.

I'm not afraid of confrontation. If I'm upset about something, I prefer to get it out in the open. If it's anger, it will blow over quickly. I don't bear grudges and I don't understand the concept of holding on to unexpressed anger. Rage, anger, frustration aren't the only emotional responses I dislike holding back.

Love, joy, excitement, anticipation, anxiety, amusement; all of these bubble out of me in a flow that can be very difficult for some people to keep up with or cope with. Mother tried desperately to teach me to withhold my emotions from others. I know this is the polite thing to do. These days I understand that most people rarely openly express how they're feeling.

Mother's punishments certainly had a lasting effect on me. I've been taught to expect punishment if I express myself too freely. So, despite the internal turmoil that results from holding back my emotions, I can be quite restrained in the company of strangers.

When I accept someone into my circle of friends or into my heart, I immediately let that façade drop away and show my characters. It's my way of telling someone I trust them. Unfortunately, many people think I'm annoyed, angry or too intensely involved with them. Intensity is something I've had to learn to measure by other people's standards. For me these rushes of emotion are normal, natural and a great release of pent-up energy. If I don't let it all out, I quickly become exhausted from the immense effort of holding back. That leads eventually to trance, shut-down or just plain rage.

I must be allowed to burn out my compulsions. I always have certain subjects I'm fascinated with. This focus of attention has shifted over the course of my life and may also shift over a short period of a few months. When I was 15 I was completely focused on the French language to the point where I became fluent in a short time. Now I could hardly string a sentence together.

I derive great satisfaction from creating beautiful things that stimulate the senses and the emotions. Creativity is my spiritual path. I used to paint a lot before I got my hands on a computer. Then I took up writing novels and designing intricate mandalas. For a long while I've been making furniture.

I love hearing stories and I love telling them. Storytelling is a spiritual practice in my opinion. In my grandparents' day – before television – stories were the way wisdom and experience got passed on from one generation to the next. Stories set the precedents and established the morality of the society. Nowadays we put old people in nursing homes and ignore the wonderful tales they have to tell of their lives. I don't understand our strange society.

As technology has advanced I've moved into music composition. Helen and I have a little home-recording studio. I spend a lot of my time composing orchestral pieces as backdrops to my life, my novels and my dreams. In my view, music is a pure form of storytelling through which I can express emotional states and experiences without the need for mere words. As I'm writing this I'm listening to some of my orchestral compositions playing through headphones. It helps me to relax and tell my story without worrying too much how you're going to judge me.

I've just started making short films to accompany my music and the next thing I'll be getting into is free podcasts of my work. In the last 12 months I've started playing the didjeridu. That's resulted in a collection of compositions that are slowly evolving into a trance album aimed at healing and calming. I'm very excited about sharing this aspect of my music.

I'm also a sculptor. I work with wood, ceramic and found objects. I make drums from goat and calf hide and I tune them to the ancient Indian musical scales, known as *ragas*. I use these drums to reach deeper states of trance where I can tap into my creativity without being interrupted by the distractions of the world.

Creativity is a kind of meditation for me – a pure, unadulterated form of meditation. If I'm travelling and I can't be involved in creative projects, I must sit quietly to meditate every day for at least an hour. If I miss two days I can become frantic, clumsy, jittery and easily distracted. Without regular meditation the world soon becomes an apparently hostile place where danger constantly lurks and fear stalks me.

Another thing I ask of anyone who comes into my circle of friends is to try to restrain a natural tendency to want to look after me. I need to be allowed to explore this world for myself. No one else can explain it to me. I simply won't understand what you're on about.

Don't worry if I seem to be making mistakes. It's very important to me to make mistakes. I learn from mistakes. In fact I learn much better if I make mistakes than if I'm simply told to accept some concept or idea. I learn by watching. Rules, morals and limitations are abstract concepts to me. I respect other people's need to maintain these structures, but unless I have practical experience of the whys and wherefores I can't be expected to stick to them.

For example, as a child I was repeatedly told I couldn't fly, but I had to jump off the balcony a hundred times before I understood this to be true. I'd seen fledgling magpies struggling to fly and I knew it could take a few tries to get right. Once I realised I couldn't learn to fly, I didn't bother trying again. I hurt myself in the process, but I was testing my limitations and that's important to me.

This method of learning about the world may sound insane to most people. But when you apply this methodology to subjects like orchestral arrangement it's obvious that I can learn by trial and error and through making mistakes. I never learned to read musical notation and I don't need to know anything about it to compose for a full orchestra.

I've learned not to trust the advice and judgements of most people. I was told by my 12th grade music teacher that I'd never be a musician. Clearly he was wrong to jump to that conclusion simply because I wasn't interested in learning musical notation. In my experience music has nothing to do with dots on a page.

Exploration of this life is what I live for. To me, spiritual exploration and learning are the only reasonable responses I can find to all the madness I see happening in the world.

I can't see any point to being alive if I'm forced into the same routines each and every day or am limited by the low expectations of others. I've had office jobs. I'm very good at filing. It's not the office work I can't stand; it's having to do the same thing day after day without much variation or any further learning.

While I need some rituals in my life to help me get things done, these little practices are more to do with a kind of auto-pilot mechanism that kicks in when I begin to trance out. I have a strict routine for cleaning my teeth. Every step must be done in a certain order or I can become quite upset. This is because I've come to use the time when this mundane task must be performed as an opportunity for trance, meditation and contemplation.

I don't like to talk while I'm engaged in my little rituals because I'm off in the Far Country and I don't want to be dragged back to the real world. I process information and learning during these rituals. I absorb my experiences and allow lessons to settle into me.

Let me sleep when I want to. Let me stay up all night watching television now and then if it makes me happy. Explain to me gently when I've offended you and you'll see I'm not a malicious person. If you tell me I'm incapable of something, I'm very likely to prove you wrong so you may as well support me in my obsession.

Don't tell me I'm a psycho – not even in jest. I'll switch you off because I don't understand what's so funny about put-downs. I see them as cruel. Don't laugh at me when I fail. I enjoy failing. It makes me look at problems from a different point of view and it helps me solve them. Criticise me, by all means. I want to be a better person and I like to consider other points of view.

When I want to be left alone, leave me alone. As Bing Crosby so eloquently put it, 'Let me be by myself in the evening breeze and listen to the murmur of the cottonwood trees. Send me off forever but I ask you please… Don't fence me in.'

I'm eccentric. I do things differently. Let me be me. There's more than one way to skin a green tree-snake. And in my experience what some people call patience others call stubbornness.

I opened this account of my life by saying that I've been a zombie and that every now and then I might snatch a brief glimpse of my surroundings through a fog of confusion. The powerful spell that bound me was brought on by abuse aimed at teaching me to conform. In certain branches of Voodoo practice there's a deep belief in zombies. When I talk about zombies I'm not referring to mythical un-dead corpses who dress in rags and feed on brains. To me a zombie is anyone who blunders through life at the whim of a sorcerer. In my understanding the sorcerer's club includes peers, parents, preachers or even society as a whole. I consider anyone who seeks to bind another into a strict or narrow conformity to be a sorcerer. For example, the world of fashion is full of zombies stumbling about in the dark snapping up whatever is marketed to them no matter how distasteful or ridiculously expensive it may be.

In a very real sense Mother tried to transform me into a conformity zombie. Her spell consisted of constant abuse aimed at beating me into shape. She wanted a worthwhile, unthinking, obedient slave who'd follow the rules and make her proud. Her inability to think outside the square caused me immense suffering and brought on a split in me. I learned to repeat the rules by rote in a trauma trance but recitation didn't teach me to live by the rules.

Someone who's been subjected to the zombie-spell of abuse can easily recognise the effects in others. I now believe that I went through all that trauma in my young life so I could be a proper support for Helen when the time came. That thought gives me a great deal of peace and puts to rest any memories of the injustices done to me as a boy. It gives me a purpose. It makes sense of everything.

All the great spiritual traditions of the world, including Christianity, teach that some good comes even from the worst excesses of evil. In that sense evil can never prevail in this world. Recently I came to understand that telling my story could benefit others. I've always wanted to be a healer.

Many of the tribal peoples of South America venerate traditional healers who are believed to be able to travel to the realm of the spirit as easily as they walk in the material world. Under the influence of the Mahjee aspect I've obsessively studied their customs. I've spoken with folks who've spent time in the rain forest of the Amazon among tribes who still preserve their ancient practices.

Diverse peoples all over the planet once held belief systems similar to the tribes of the Amazon. The practice of walking between the worlds of spirit and matter is referred to by anthropologists as shamanism, from the anglicised Siberian word for such a person – shaman. I'll use that word from here on to simplify things.

In South America the steps toward becoming a shaman are clearly delineated. First, an elder shaman will recognise a gifted youth as being a future shaman. There are signs to look out for such as a deep fascination with exploring the world. A profound sensitivity. An unusual degree of empathy which may appear to be a psychic ability to those who don't understand it. An affinity with rhythm, music and trance.

Once he's discovered an apprentice, the elder will train him or her in all the practical knowledge of healing – the herbs and remedies of the forest. Over many years the elder will gradually reveal the deeper secrets of the spirit-realm to the apprentice. At some point when the elder considers his student is ready there will be an initiation into the deeper mysteries of life.

Traditional societies have quite different interpretations of this opening ritual and it takes many forms. Among some tribes a hallucinogenic drug made from sacred plants of the forest is used to allow the apprentice to view the world differently and to see spirits. Drugs aren't used recreationally in these tribes; they're specifically administered for healing purposes. In other cultures drumming, fasting or feats of physical endurance open the door to the other world.

However, almost every society that venerates the path of the shaman shares some common features of the initiation process. At some point during the ritual celebrations the student enters into the spirit world of trance and leaves the material world behind. In that trance state the trainee shaman is introduced to his spirit guides and assured he is being well taken care of. A guide may appear to take the form of an animal, a strange man or wild woman. The guide may be an ancestor or an archetypal being such as a dragon or a raven. There may be several guides who present themselves. The student often sees himself as a spirit being and may assume the form of an animal, bird or man.

Every culture has its own subtle variations on the theme of the shamanic journey into the spirit world of trance. Another thing they all have in common is a vivid dream or vision in which the initiate is symbolically dismembered and their body is metaphorically ripped to pieces. The guides will then calmly put the new shaman back together to show him he has nothing to fear from the experience of death.

When I first heard about these traditions from an acquaintance who'd lived in the Amazon, I became fascinated with the vision of destruction and resurrection of the body. At the time I didn't understand why it touched me so deeply; I just wanted to know more about this concept.

I've been through so much in my life but I've always known I was on a spiritual quest, even if it didn't always seem to be the major priority in my life. It was only very recently that I realised I'd been torn apart by the abuse that Mother and Father inflicted on me as a child.

Perhaps because I'm an autistic person who is extremely sensitive and emotional, the trauma of that abuse affected me all the more profoundly. Lately I've found myself wondering whether or not dissociative identity disorder is similar to the vivid shamanic vision of having one's body torn to pieces. I'm not trying to make out that I'm some sort of guru or anything special; that's not what I'm on about at all. I'm just trying to make sense of everything that happened to me.

Whether it be the tribes of the Amazon or the Pitjantjatjara people of Central Australia there is a shared belief among all the ancient cultures in a spirit-realm beyond the perception of the ordinary senses of human beings. The peoples of this planet who are not wealth-oriented acknowledge there are some among their number who can walk in the spirit world and return to speak of the things they have learned there.

I can't lay claim to any authentic shamanic initiation, but I can say that I've been through an awful lot in my lifetime. Whether it be through pure good fortune or, as I believe, because some spirit guide was watching over me and pushing me in the right direction, I've survived.

I didn't have an elder to teach me. I didn't have a family who were willing to support me in my disability. So I was forced to turn my disability into an asset. I didn't always succeed. I've made plenty of mistakes along the way. But I believe that I've learned more from my mistakes than I could have done by sitting at home safe and warm where nothing could harm me. I thank my parents for being the bloody dickheads they were. I thank them for their narrow-minded bigotry and their simple belief that I could be cured of my problems with a damn good thrashing. Their misguided methods made me who I am today. So I find it easy to forgive them.

I've had to find some peace with the past before the next part of the healing journey could begin. Recently Helen and I were watching a documentary about autism. I heard the autistic author and advocate Donna Williams speaking about her life. I went to look at her website later that night and I was surprised that our lives had been so similar. I wrote her a quick e-mail thanking her for speaking out so bravely about herself. One thing led to another. I was asked to dust off the original manuscript of my autobiography and re-read it.

I'd given up on being an author. It was just too difficult and my confidence had been shattered by my experiences of the business of publishing. However, Donna convinced me that I could actually do a lot of good by sharing my story and that inspired me to rewrite this book from start to finish. I hope I can make a difference with it.

Recently Donna spoke to me about her ticks and twitches. She asked me about mine. I was so confronted I simply went along with the conversation and tried not to show how distressed I was. I've spent a lifetime hiding my ticks, keeping them to myself and only letting them manifest when I knew I was alone. Even Helen hasn't seen them very often. It's extremely upsetting for me to be so open about something I've had to cover up for so long. Marco Polo doesn't like that sort of exposure.

He likes drums. So, to placate him I've taken up making drums. They're drums for dancing, drums for entering trance and for calming the spirits of those who need rhythm in their lives to soothe them.

I've made the decision to live without relying on medication to keep me calm. I've looked into all the alternatives and I'm sure I'd prefer to go without pharmaceuticals for as long as possible. The side-effects are worse than any benefits, to my way of thinking. But living without medication requires vigilance, self-discipline and determination.

Helen and I have taken up going to the sweat-house. We try to attend two sweat lodges a year if we can. We sweat out the toxins and talk about our life journey with others in the darkness of the lodge. I love the thought of sharing an experience that probably hasn't changed in hundreds of generations, even though Westerners rarely get the opportunity to take part in it these days. For city dwellers it's easy to forget that fire, water, earth and air are the very essence of all things. The sweat-house is where I go to remember what I'm made of.

The only advice I have to offer for those non-autistics who are struggling to understand an autistic person is: try to be patient with them. Try to understand that there are many ways to perceive the world; each of them is just as valid as the other. Compassion. Acceptance. Love. These are the qualities that foster the only healing worth having.

As I said earlier, in many traditional societies people who are gifted with highly attuned senses and intense emotional experiences were respected for the different view they offer of life. They are shamans, seers and guides. There may not seem to be much of a place for such people in the modern world, but I think it's time we acknowledged the worth of everyone and stopped talking in terms of disorders. As if any of us could ever live up to the strict definitions of what is normal. As if.

Psychologists tell me that autism rarely manifests alone. There's usually some other disorder or anxiety connected with it. That's only natural considering it can be such an intense path in life. In my case post-traumatic shock and the associated shame became a dragon at my shoulder. I like to say that if autism is my blessing then the shame-dragon has been my curse. What I mean is that post-traumatic stress and DID have been a counterbalance to the very positive aspects of autism. At last, in my forties, I can begin to feel that the blessing outweighs the curse. I have come to see my life as a long initiation similar to that which eventually transforms an apprentice into a shaman.

I've got a long way to go yet on my pilgrimage and a lot more to learn as well. I intend to go off into the Amazon rainforest and take an initiation when the time is right. My entire life seems to have been preparing me for just such an experience. And I have a sense the changing world needs more shamans in these troubled times when our entire species seems to have gone mad with materialism.

I'm now learning to forgive myself for being autistic, strange, retarded, psychotic, traumatised and mentally defective. I'm learning to accept myself. I'm throwing off the prejudiced view I was taught to hold of myself. Perhaps in time this splintered soul will return to the One.

At the end of the day I believe we all have to count our blessings. I've been given many and I want to go on sharing them with the world. A psychologist told me a short while ago that I have a remarkable and rare ability to turn a negative into a positive. I suppose I've always been an optimist. Thank goodness.